Trumpisms: Decoding the Rhetoric of Disruption

Adrian Rocquecliffe

Published by Writers Sidekick Publishing, 2024.

TRUMPISMS: DECODING THE RHETORIC OF DISRUPTION

First edition. August 30, 2024.

ISBN: 979-8227010513

Written by Adrian Rocquecliffe.

Introduction

During his tenure as President of the United States, Donald Trump was known for his distinctive communication style, often using direct, unfiltered statements that came to be widely recognized as "Trumpisms." These remarks, characterized by their boldness and simplicity, were not just typical political rhetoric; they were potent expressions that defined his leadership and resonated deeply with his base, while frequently sparking debate and controversy among critics and the broader public.

"Trumpisms" often involved sweeping assertions about his administration's achievements in areas such as the economy, military, and foreign policy, as well as bold claims about historical comparisons—asserting, for example, that no president had done more for specific demographic groups or policy areas than he had. These statements were frequently presented in superlative terms, suggesting unparalleled success across various fronts of his presidency.

This collection aims to explore some of the most emblematic "Trumpisms," providing not only the context in which they were made but also a detailed analysis to assess their factual accuracy. Each entry scrutinizes the original remark, offers the date and setting in which it was delivered, and provides a response that dissects the hyperbole to reveal the underlying facts. By doing so, we aim to illuminate the strategies behind his communication, understand the factual basis of his claims, and consider their impact on American public discourse and policy during his administration.

Understanding these "Trumpisms" is crucial for grasping the dynamics of Trump's policy communication, the political climate of his presidency, and the ways in which his words have shaped public understanding and opinion in significant areas of American life. This analysis not only contributes to a more nuanced understanding of his presidency but also helps in appreciating the complex relationship between political leadership, media representation, and public perception in contemporary U.S. politics.

"Trumpisms"

Trumpism: "The concept of global warming was created by and for the Chinese in order to make U.S. manufacturing non-competitive."

- **Date:** November 6, 2012
- **Situation:** Tweet by Donald Trump
- **Correct Response:** Climate change is a global issue recognized by the vast majority of scientists as caused by human activities, not by any specific country for economic reasons.

Trumpism: "We had the greatest economy in the history of our country."

- **Date:** Various speeches and rallies throughout 2020
- **Situation:** Campaign speeches and rallies
- **Correct Response:** While the U.S. economy was strong in early 2020, it wasn't the greatest in history. Economic measures like GDP growth, unemployment rates, and stock market performance need to be compared across different periods, and several other periods in U.S. history had similar or better economic indicators.

Trumpism: "We built the wall."

- **Date:** February 4, 2020
- **Situation:** State of the Union address
- **Correct Response:** While some wall construction and repairs occurred during Trump's presidency, the promise of a full wall along the southern border was not completed, with only a portion of the wall built.

Trumpism: "We're the highest stock market in history."

- **Date:** January 9, 2020
- **Situation:** Speech at a rally in Toledo, Ohio

- **Correct Response:** While the stock market did reach record highs during Trump's presidency, stock market performance fluctuates and is influenced by many factors. The stock market is not the sole indicator of economic health, and it does not reflect the economic experiences of all Americans, especially those not invested in stocks.

Trumpism: "There were very fine people on both sides."

- **Date:** August 15, 2017
- **Situation:** Press conference discussing the Charlottesville rally
- **Correct Response:** This comment was widely criticized because it appeared to equate white supremacists with those protesting against them. In reality, one side was advocating racist ideologies, while the other side was opposing these beliefs.

Trumpism: "The U.S. has the cleanest air in the world."

- **Date:** September 26, 2019
- **Situation:** Speech at the United Nations General Assembly
- **Correct Response:** While the U.S. has made progress in air quality, it is not the cleanest in the world. Countries like Finland, Iceland, and Sweden have cleaner air, according to the World Health Organization.

Trumpism: "We have it totally under control. It's one person coming in from China."

- **Date:** January 22, 2020
- **Situation:** Interview with CNBC about COVID-19
- **Correct Response:** This statement was made at the beginning of the COVID-19 pandemic, which later spread widely across the U.S. and the world. The virus was not under control at that time, and it required significant public health efforts to manage the

spread.

Trumpism: "I know more about ISIS than the generals do, believe me."

- **Date:** November 12, 2015
- **Situation:** Campaign rally in Fort Dodge, Iowa
- **Correct Response:** Military generals and intelligence officials dedicate their careers to studying and combating threats like ISIS. This statement exaggerates Trump's knowledge and diminishes the expertise of experienced military leaders.

Trumpism: "The Mueller Report totally exonerated me."

- **Date:** March 24, 2019
- **Situation:** Statement to reporters after the release of the Mueller Report summary
- **Correct Response:** The Mueller Report explicitly stated that it did not exonerate Trump of obstruction of justice. The report detailed multiple instances where Trump may have obstructed justice but left the final judgment to Congress.

Trumpism: "We've ended the war on beautiful clean coal."

- **Date:** June 1, 2017
- **Situation:** Announcement of the U.S. withdrawal from the Paris Climate Agreement
- **Correct Response:** While Trump aimed to boost the coal industry, "clean coal" is a term often criticized as misleading. Coal is a significant contributor to pollution and carbon emissions, and its decline is more tied to market forces and the rise of cheaper, cleaner energy sources like natural gas and renewables.

Trumpism: "We're building the wall, and Mexico is paying for it."

- **Date:** Multiple occasions, notably during the 2016 campaign
- **Situation:** Campaign promise
- **Correct Response:** Mexico did not pay for the wall. The U.S. government funded the portions of the wall that were constructed, primarily through reallocated funds from the Defense Department.

Trumpism: "I inherited a mess. It's a mess. At home and abroad, a mess."

- **Date:** February 16, 2017
- **Situation:** Press conference at the White House
- **Correct Response:** While every administration inherits challenges, Trump's claim oversimplifies the situation. The U.S. economy was in recovery, with low unemployment and steady growth, when Trump took office. International relations were also complex but not uniformly a "mess."

Trumpism: "Hillary Clinton started the birther controversy. I finished it."

- **Date:** September 16, 2016
- **Situation:** Campaign speech in Washington, D.C.
- **Correct Response:** The birther movement, which falsely claimed President Obama was not born in the U.S., was promoted by Trump himself, not Hillary Clinton. The claim that Clinton started it is inaccurate and has been debunked by multiple fact-checkers.

Trumpism: "The election was rigged."

- **Date:** November 4, 2020, and repeatedly after
- **Situation:** Post-election claims about the 2020 presidential election
- **Correct Response:** Multiple audits, recounts, and court rulings

confirmed that the 2020 election was fair and that there was no widespread voter fraud. These claims were repeatedly dismissed by election officials and courts across the political spectrum.

Trumpism: "The coronavirus is going to disappear. One day, it's like a miracle—it will disappear."

- **Date:** February 28, 2020
- **Situation:** Remarks at a White House event
- **Correct Response:** The COVID-19 pandemic did not simply "disappear." It required extensive public health measures, including vaccines, social distancing, and mask-wearing, to control its spread. The virus continued to affect millions of people worldwide long after this statement was made.

Trumpism: "We have the best [COVID-19] testing in the world."

- **Date:** May 11, 2020
- **Situation:** Press briefing at the White House
- **Correct Response:** While the U.S. ramped up COVID-19 testing efforts, early in the pandemic, the country faced significant testing shortages and delays. Many other countries were able to implement widespread and rapid testing more efficiently, highlighting challenges in the U.S. response.

Trumpism: "Windmills cause cancer."

- **Date:** April 2, 2019
- **Situation:** Remarks at a National Republican Congressional Committee dinner
- **Correct Response:** There is no scientific evidence to support the claim that wind turbines cause cancer. This statement is an example of misinformation that misrepresents the safety and environmental benefits of wind energy.

Trumpism: "The noise [from wind turbines] causes cancer."

- **Date:** April 2, 2019
- **Situation:** Remarks at a National Republican Congressional Committee dinner
- **Correct Response:** This claim has no scientific basis. Wind turbines do not emit noise levels that would cause cancer or any other major health issues, according to health experts and studies.

Trumpism: "I've had the most successful first two years of any president."

- **Date:** February 5, 2019
- **Situation:** State of the Union address
- **Correct Response:** Success in a presidency is subjective and can be measured in many ways. While Trump passed significant tax reforms and appointed Supreme Court justices, other presidents, such as Franklin D. Roosevelt during the Great Depression, also had highly impactful first terms. Many historians and political analysts would argue that Trump's claim is exaggerated.

Trumpism: "Our military is completely depleted."

- **Date:** September 7, 2016
- **Situation:** Remarks at the Commander-in-Chief Forum
- **Correct Response:** The U.S. military was not "completely depleted" before Trump took office. The military continued to be one of the most powerful and well-funded in the world. While there were calls for increased defense spending, the statement overstated the situation.

Trumpism: "The whistleblower got it all wrong."

- **Date:** September 24, 2019
- **Situation:** Remarks following the release of the whistleblower

complaint during the Ukraine scandal

- **Correct Response:** The whistleblower's complaint about Trump's phone call with Ukraine's president was largely corroborated by multiple witnesses during the impeachment inquiry. The complaint was not "all wrong" but rather aligned with the findings of subsequent investigations.

Trumpism: "I will be proud to shut down the government for border security."

- **Date:** December 11, 2018
- **Situation:** Meeting with Nancy Pelosi and Chuck Schumer in the Oval Office
- **Correct Response:** The government shutdown that followed lasted 35 days, the longest in U.S. history. It caused significant disruption and hardship for federal employees and contractors, many of whom went without pay during the shutdown. The shutdown did not lead to the full funding or construction of the border wall as initially demanded.

Trumpism: "We're the highest taxed nation in the world."

- **Date:** Multiple occasions during 2016-2017
- **Situation:** Campaign rallies and speeches
- **Correct Response:** The U.S. is not the highest taxed nation in the world. According to the Organization for Economic Cooperation and Development (OECD), the U.S. has a lower tax burden compared to many developed countries, particularly in Europe.

Trumpism: "The U.S. steel industry is dead."

- **Date:** March 1, 2018
- **Situation:** Announcement of tariffs on steel and aluminum
- **Correct Response:** While the U.S. steel industry has faced

challenges, it was not "dead." The industry was still producing steel and employed tens of thousands of workers. The tariffs imposed by Trump were intended to boost the industry, but the claim of its death was an exaggeration.

Trumpism: "The Russia investigation is a witch hunt."

- **Date:** Multiple occasions from 2017-2019
- **Situation:** Tweets and public statements regarding the Mueller investigation
- **Correct Response:** The Mueller investigation resulted in numerous indictments, guilty pleas, and convictions of Trump associates. It uncovered extensive evidence of Russian interference in the 2016 election, though it did not conclude that Trump conspired with Russia. The investigation was not baseless but grounded in credible evidence.

Trumpism: "Herd mentality is going to develop. It's going to be herd-developed, and that's going to happen."

- **Date:** September 15, 2020
- **Situation:** Town hall meeting with ABC News
- **Correct Response:** Trump likely meant to refer to "herd immunity," a concept where enough of the population becomes immune to a disease, making its spread unlikely. The term "herd mentality" refers to people following the crowd without critical thinking, which is unrelated to public health. Herd immunity for COVID-19 was not achievable without significant loss of life or widespread vaccination, making the statement misleading.

Trumpism: "I don't think science knows, actually."

- **Date:** September 14, 2020
- **Situation:** Remarks during a visit to California amid wildfires

- **Correct Response:** This comment was made in response to scientific warnings about climate change's role in worsening wildfires. The overwhelming majority of climate scientists agree that human-caused climate change is contributing to more severe and frequent wildfires. The statement undermines established scientific consensus.

Trumpism: "The U.S. has among the lowest [COVID-19] mortality rates in the world."

- **Date:** July 21, 2020
- **Situation:** Interview with Fox News
- **Correct Response:** At the time, the U.S. had one of the highest COVID-19 death tolls in the world, both in absolute numbers and per capita. The statement was misleading, as many other countries had significantly lower mortality rates due to more effective pandemic responses.

Trumpism: "You had very fine people on both sides."

- **Date:** August 15, 2017
- **Situation:** Press conference following the Charlottesville rally
- **Correct Response:** This comment equated white supremacists and neo-Nazis with those protesting against them, causing widespread outrage. It ignored the violent and racist nature of one side and was seen as a false equivalence.

Trumpism: "If we didn't do any testing, we would have very few cases."

- **Date:** June 15, 2020
- **Situation:** Roundtable discussion with restaurant executives
- **Correct Response:** Testing does not create COVID-19 cases; it identifies them. The number of cases reflects the spread of the virus, not the amount of testing. Reducing testing would not reduce

actual infections; it would simply hide the true scale of the outbreak.

Trumpism: "The Kurds are much safer right now, but the Kurds know how to fight, and as I said, they're not angels."

- **Date:** October 16, 2019
- **Situation:** Press conference following the decision to withdraw U.S. troops from northern Syria
- **Correct Response:** The decision to withdraw U.S. troops led to a Turkish military offensive against the Kurdish forces, who were key allies in the fight against ISIS. This move was widely criticized for abandoning the Kurds, leading to significant violence and displacement. The statement downplayed the consequences of the withdrawal.

Trumpism: "I have the absolute right to do what I want with the Justice Department."

- **Date:** December 28, 2017
- **Situation:** Interview with The New York Times
- **Correct Response:** While the president has significant influence over the Justice Department, it is meant to operate with a degree of independence to ensure the fair and impartial application of the law. The statement raised concerns about potential abuses of power and undermining the rule of law.

Trumpism: "Nobody ever knew health care could be so complicated."

- **Date:** February 27, 2017
- **Situation:** Meeting with governors
- **Correct Response:** Health care policy is widely known to be complex, involving a wide range of issues from insurance markets to public health. Experts and policymakers have long recognized

the challenges in reforming the health care system, making this statement seem out of touch with the reality of the issue.

Trumpism: "I alone can fix it."

- **Date:** July 21, 2016
- **Situation:** Republican National Convention speech
- **Correct Response:** Effective governance typically requires collaboration, checks and balances, and input from various stakeholders, not the actions of a single individual. This statement was criticized for its authoritarian tone and misunderstanding of democratic processes.

Trumpism: "People are flushing toilets 10 times, 15 times, as opposed to once."

- **Date:** December 6, 2019
- **Situation:** Roundtable discussion with small business leaders
- **Correct Response:** There is no widespread evidence that people need to flush toilets multiple times as described. This claim seemed to exaggerate issues with water efficiency standards and was widely mocked as out of touch with real concerns.

Trumpism: "We have the cleanest water we've ever had."

- **Date:** June 30, 2020
- **Situation:** Remarks at a White House event
- **Correct Response:** While the U.S. has made significant progress in water quality over the years, the statement overlooks ongoing challenges with water pollution and contamination, such as lead in drinking water in Flint, Michigan, and other areas. It also fails to acknowledge that clean water standards were established long before Trump's presidency.

Trumpism: "We're very close to a vaccine."

- **Date:** March 2, 2020
- **Situation:** Meeting with pharmaceutical executives at the White House
- **Correct Response:** At the time of this statement, a COVID-19 vaccine was not "very close." Vaccine development typically takes years, and while the COVID-19 vaccines were developed at unprecedented speed, they were not available until late 2020 and early 2021.

Trumpism: "I think I've done more for the Black community than any other president, and let's take a pass on Abraham Lincoln."

- **Date:** October 22, 2020
- **Situation:** Final presidential debate with Joe Biden
- **Correct Response:** While Trump's administration implemented some policies that affected the Black community, such as criminal justice reform, many historians argue that other presidents, particularly Abraham Lincoln, who signed the Emancipation Proclamation, and Lyndon B. Johnson, who passed civil rights legislation, had a more profound impact.

Trumpism: "We're not going to lose any [COVID-19] cases. It's going to be down to close to zero."

- **Date:** February 26, 2020
- **Situation:** Press briefing at the White House
- **Correct Response:** The number of COVID-19 cases did not go "down to close to zero." Instead, the virus spread rapidly across the U.S. and the world, leading to millions of cases and deaths. This statement greatly underestimated the severity of the pandemic.

Trumpism: "Puerto Rico got $91 billion for the hurricane."

- **Date:** April 2, 2019
- **Situation:** Remarks during a meeting with Republican senators
- **Correct Response:** The $91 billion figure was inaccurate. The actual amount allocated for Puerto Rico's recovery after Hurricane Maria was much lower, and the disbursement of funds faced significant delays. The figure cited by Trump included future projections of expenses, which were not immediate or guaranteed.

Trumpism: "We're building a wall in Colorado."

- **Date:** October 23, 2019
- **Situation:** Remarks at a speech in Pittsburgh
- **Correct Response:** Colorado does not share a border with Mexico, making it an unlikely location for a border wall. This statement was widely mocked and clarified later as a mistake, with Trump saying he meant the wall would indirectly benefit Colorado.

Trumpism: "We're going to have insurance for everybody."

- **Date:** January 15, 2017
- **Situation:** Interview with The Washington Post
- **Correct Response:** The proposed health care policies under Trump's administration, particularly efforts to repeal the Affordable Care Act (ACA), were projected to result in millions losing their health insurance. "Insurance for everybody" was not achieved during his term.

Trumpism: "The United States has among the lowest [COVID-19] mortality rates in the world."

- **Date:** July 21, 2020
- **Situation:** Interview with Fox News
- **Correct Response:** At the time, the U.S. had one of the highest

COVID-19 death tolls both in absolute numbers and per capita. This statement was misleading, as many other countries had significantly lower mortality rates due to more effective pandemic responses.

Trumpism: "It's one person coming in from China. We have it under control."

- **Date:** January 22, 2020
- **Situation:** Interview with CNBC about COVID-19
- **Correct Response:** This statement underestimated the spread and severity of COVID-19. The virus rapidly spread globally, leading to a pandemic that required extensive public health measures to control. The situation was not under control at the time of this statement.

Trumpism: "You know, we should go back to election night. We should go back to election night, because what happened was Donald Trump was winning by a lot, and then all of a sudden, it was just called off."

- **Date:** December 2, 2020
- **Situation:** Remarks in a 46-minute video address
- **Correct Response:** Votes are counted after Election Day, and the apparent shift in results as more votes are counted is a normal part of the process. There was no evidence to support claims that the election results were "called off" or changed inappropriately. The 2020 election results were certified as fair and accurate.

Trumpism: "We have tremendous African American support. I would say I'm at my all-time high."

- **Date:** June 5, 2020
- **Situation:** Remarks at a roundtable with law enforcement officials
- **Correct Response:** Polling data consistently showed that Trump's

support among African American voters was relatively low compared to other groups. This statement exaggerated his level of support among this demographic.

Trumpism: "Our GDP is higher than that of any other country in the world."

- **Date:** June 18, 2020
- **Situation:** Remarks at a campaign rally in Tulsa, Oklahoma
- **Correct Response:** While the U.S. has one of the largest economies in the world, GDP growth rates vary by country. This statement was misleading, as it conflates overall GDP size with growth rates and does not account for different economic conditions across nations.

Trumpism: "We passed Veterans Choice. It was passed by us, but it was actually never used."

- **Date:** August 21, 2020
- **Situation:** Remarks at a rally in Arlington, Virginia
- **Correct Response:** The Veterans Choice Program was signed into law by President Obama in 2014. While Trump signed the VA MISSION Act in 2018, which expanded the program, he did not create it, as this statement implies.

Trumpism: "We have more cases because we have more testing."

- **Date:** June 15, 2020
- **Situation:** Remarks at a roundtable with restaurant executives
- **Correct Response:** Testing does not create cases; it identifies them. The number of cases reflects the actual spread of the virus, not just the amount of testing. This statement misrepresented the relationship between testing and case numbers.

Trumpism: "The wall is going up faster than anyone ever imagined."

- **Date:** September 25, 2019
- **Situation:** Speech at the United Nations General Assembly
- **Correct Response:** While some sections of the border wall were built or replaced, much of the construction involved replacing existing barriers rather than building new ones. The statement exaggerated the speed and extent of wall construction.

Trumpism: "We're the only country in the world where a person comes in, has a baby, and the baby is essentially a citizen of the United States."

- **Date:** October 30, 2018
- **Situation:** Interview with Axios on HBO
- **Correct Response:** The U.S. is not the only country with birthright citizenship. Over 30 countries, including Canada and most Latin American nations, grant automatic citizenship to babies born on their soil, making this statement inaccurate.

Trumpism: "You can do anything. Grab them by the [expletive]."

- **Date:** October 7, 2005 (released in 2016)
- **Situation:** Leaked Access Hollywood tape
- **Correct Response:** This statement, which Trump dismissed as "locker room talk," was widely condemned as promoting sexual assault. It led to significant backlash, particularly regarding attitudes towards women and consent.

Trumpism: "The new trade deal is the biggest trade deal in the history of our country."

- **Date:** October 1, 2018
- **Situation:** Announcement of the United States-Mexico-Canada Agreement (USMCA)

- **Correct Response:** While the USMCA updated and replaced NAFTA, it was not the largest trade deal in U.S. history. Other trade agreements, such as the Trans-Pacific Partnership (which the U.S. withdrew from), involved more countries and covered a larger share of global trade.

Trumpism: "The Mueller report totally exonerates me."

- **Date:** March 24, 2019
- **Situation:** Remarks following the release of Attorney General William Barr's summary of the Mueller report
- **Correct Response:** The Mueller report explicitly stated that it did not exonerate Trump, particularly regarding obstruction of justice. The report found insufficient evidence to charge Trump with collusion with Russia but left open the question of obstruction, contrary to Trump's claim.

Trumpism: "My father gave me a small loan of a million dollars."

- **Date:** October 26, 2015
- **Situation:** Interview on The Tonight Show Starring Jimmy Fallon
- **Correct Response:** A loan of $1 million is not considered small by most standards, especially at the time Trump received it. Furthermore, Trump later inherited much more from his father, with some estimates suggesting he received over $400 million, significantly more than a "small loan."

Trumpism: "I think that climate change is a hoax."

- **Date:** November 6, 2012
- **Situation:** Tweet
- **Correct Response:** The overwhelming consensus among climate scientists is that climate change is real and primarily driven by human activities, particularly the burning of fossil fuels. This

statement dismisses well-established scientific evidence.

Trumpism: "I've been involved in a lot of lawsuits. They're fun."

- **Date:** October 13, 2016
- **Situation:** Remarks at a campaign rally in West Palm Beach, Florida
- **Correct Response:** Lawsuits are serious legal matters, often involving significant financial, emotional, and time costs. Describing them as "fun" trivializes the impact they can have on individuals and businesses.

Trumpism: "I was the person who saved Pre-Existing Conditions in your Healthcare."

- **Date:** October 15, 2020
- **Situation:** Tweet
- **Correct Response:** Protections for pre-existing conditions were established under the Affordable Care Act (ACA), signed into law by President Obama in 2010. Trump's administration attempted to repeal the ACA, which would have removed these protections, making this claim misleading.

Trumpism: "The biggest tax cut in history."

- **Date:** December 20, 2017
- **Situation:** Remarks on the Tax Cuts and Jobs Act
- **Correct Response:** The Tax Cuts and Jobs Act of 2017 was one of the largest tax cuts in U.S. history, but not the absolute largest. Adjusted for inflation, earlier tax cuts, such as those implemented during World War II, were larger in real terms.

Trumpism: "We've had the best economy ever."

- **Date:** Multiple occasions, particularly in 2018 and 2019
- **Situation:** Various speeches and interviews
- **Correct Response:** While the economy experienced growth during Trump's presidency, other periods in U.S. history had higher GDP growth rates and lower unemployment. Claims of the "best economy ever" overlook the broader historical context.

Trumpism: "I don't know much about David Duke, but I know he's a big Trump supporter."

- **Date:** February 28, 2016
- **Situation:** Interview on CNN
- **Correct Response:** David Duke, a former Grand Wizard of the Ku Klux Klan, was a prominent supporter of Trump's candidacy. Trump's claim of not knowing much about Duke was criticized as a failure to address or condemn his extremist support.

Trumpism: "We have a tremendous number of ventilators. We have more than we need."

- **Date:** March 30, 2020
- **Situation:** Press briefing at the White House
- **Correct Response:** Early in the pandemic, there was a significant shortage of ventilators, leading to critical shortages in some hospitals. The statement did not accurately reflect the situation, where many areas were struggling with shortages of essential medical equipment.

Trumpism: "We're working on a plan to make American manufacturing great again."

- **Date:** July 24, 2017
- **Situation:** Remarks on trade and manufacturing policy
- **Correct Response:** While Trump promoted policies aimed at

boosting American manufacturing, such as tariffs and trade deals, the effectiveness of these measures in revitalizing manufacturing was debated. Manufacturing jobs continued to face challenges during his presidency.

Trumpism: "The press is the enemy of the people."

- **Date:** February 17, 2017
- **Situation:** Tweet
- **Correct Response:** Labeling the press as the "enemy of the people" was widely criticized for undermining press freedom and promoting hostility towards journalism. The statement was seen as an attack on the role of a free press in democratic societies.

Trumpism: "The United States has the cleanest air in the world."

- **Date:** November 4, 2019
- **Situation:** Remarks at a rally
- **Correct Response:** Air quality in the U.S. has improved over the decades, but it is not the cleanest in the world. Several countries, particularly in Northern Europe, have lower levels of air pollution. This statement overlooks ongoing environmental challenges.

Trumpism: "We have the best healthcare system in the world."

- **Date:** January 10, 2020
- **Situation:** Remarks during a speech on health care
- **Correct Response:** The U.S. healthcare system has many strengths but also faces significant challenges, including high costs, lack of universal coverage, and disparities in access and outcomes. Many countries with universal healthcare systems have better overall health outcomes and lower costs.

Trumpism: "I'm the least racist person in this room."

- **Date:** July 14, 2019
- **Situation:** Remarks at a press conference following accusations of racism
- **Correct Response:** This statement was criticized as dismissive and self-serving. Accusations of racist comments and policies during Trump's presidency included his remarks about minority groups and his handling of racial issues, making this assertion controversial and disputed.

Trumpism: "The economy is the best it's ever been for minorities."

- **Date:** February 28, 2020
- **Situation:** Remarks during a speech
- **Correct Response:** While unemployment rates for minority groups did drop during Trump's presidency, they had been decreasing steadily before his term. Additionally, disparities in income and wealth persisted, and the COVID-19 pandemic disproportionately affected minority communities.

Trumpism: "The Democrats want to take your guns away."

- **Date:** October 2, 2018
- **Situation:** Remarks at a rally
- **Correct Response:** While some Democrats advocate for stricter gun control measures, no mainstream Democratic platform advocates for the complete confiscation of firearms. This statement was often used to stoke fear and mobilize supporters rather than accurately represent policy positions.

Trumpism: "I know more about technology than anyone else."

- **Date:** September 13, 2016
- **Situation:** Remarks during a campaign rally
- **Correct Response:** This statement was criticized for its

exaggeration, as Trump's public knowledge of technology and his administration's approach to tech issues did not consistently demonstrate deep expertise in the field.

Trumpism: "We've had the most successful presidency in the history of the United States."

- **Date:** August 6, 2020
- **Situation:** Interview with Fox News
- **Correct Response:** Evaluations of presidential success are subjective and vary based on criteria such as economic performance, foreign policy achievements, and historical impact. Many historians and analysts disagree with this assessment, citing various controversies and challenges during Trump's presidency.

Trumpism: "There was no collusion with Russia."

- **Date:** April 18, 2019
- **Situation:** Remarks following the release of the Mueller report
- **Correct Response:** While the Mueller report did not establish criminal conspiracy, it documented numerous contacts between Trump's campaign and Russian officials, and it found evidence of attempts to obstruct justice. The statement oversimplified the findings of the investigation.

Trumpism: "I saved the auto industry."

- **Date:** March 30, 2018
- **Situation:** Remarks at a campaign rally
- **Correct Response:** The auto industry bailout was initiated under President George W. Bush and continued under President Obama. While Trump supported some policies affecting the industry, claiming credit for its recovery overlooks the significant actions taken by previous administrations.

Trumpism: "We're going to have a fantastic trade deal with China."

- **Date:** January 15, 2020
- **Situation:** Remarks on the Phase One trade deal with China
- **Correct Response:** The Phase One trade deal with China addressed some trade issues but left many unresolved. The economic impact and effectiveness of the deal were debated, and tensions between the two countries continued beyond its signing.

Trumpism: "The Mueller investigation was a hoax."

- **Date:** March 24, 2019
- **Situation:** Remarks following the release of the Mueller report summary
- **Correct Response:** The Mueller investigation was a legitimate inquiry into Russian interference in the 2016 election and potential obstruction of justice. While Trump and his allies labeled it a "hoax," the investigation uncovered substantial evidence and led to significant legal and political consequences.

Trumpism: "The U.S. has the lowest crime rate in the world."

- **Date:** August 29, 2019
- **Situation:** Remarks at a campaign rally
- **Correct Response:** The U.S. does not have the lowest crime rate globally. Countries like Japan and several Scandinavian nations have lower crime rates. Crime rates in the U.S. are high compared to many other developed countries.

Trumpism: "We have more testing than any other country in the world."

- **Date:** May 7, 2020
- **Situation:** Press briefing at the White House
- **Correct Response:** While the U.S. conducted a large number of

COVID-19 tests, other countries, such as South Korea and Germany, also had extensive testing programs. The U.S. faced challenges with testing availability and accuracy, especially in the early stages of the pandemic.

Trumpism: "The trade deficit with China is down."

- **Date:** November 20, 2019
- **Situation:** Remarks on U.S.-China trade relations
- **Correct Response:** The trade deficit with China remained high despite the Phase One trade deal and other economic policies. The trade deficit fluctuated but did not show a significant long-term decrease during Trump's presidency.

Trumpism: "The economy is growing at an unprecedented rate."

- **Date:** March 12, 2019
- **Situation:** Remarks during a speech on economic performance
- **Correct Response:** Economic growth during Trump's presidency was strong but not unprecedented. Growth rates were similar to those experienced during previous administrations and were impacted by various factors, including tax cuts and trade policies.

Trumpism: "I'm a great president for the LGBTQ community."

- **Date:** February 25, 2020
- **Situation:** Remarks during a campaign rally
- **Correct Response:** Trump's administration faced criticism from LGBTQ advocates due to policies perceived as regressive, such as restrictions on transgender individuals serving in the military and changes to non-discrimination protections.

Trumpism: "The media is the enemy of the American people."

- **Date:** February 17, 2017
- **Situation:** Tweet
- **Correct Response:** This statement was criticized for undermining press freedom and democracy. The media plays a critical role in holding power to account, and labeling it as an "enemy" was seen as harmful to democratic institutions.

Trumpism: "We're going to see the biggest tax cuts in history."

- **Date:** September 29, 2017
- **Situation:** Remarks on tax reform
- **Correct Response:** The Tax Cuts and Jobs Act of 2017 was significant, but not the largest tax cut in U.S. history when adjusted for inflation. Previous tax cuts, including those during World War II, were larger in real terms.

Trumpism: "There was no quid pro quo."

- **Date:** September 25, 2019
- **Situation:** Remarks following the release of the Ukraine call transcript
- **Correct Response:** The claim of "no quid pro quo" was contested. The transcript of the call with Ukrainian President Zelensky indicated discussions about withholding military aid, which led to accusations of a quid pro quo arrangement.

Trumpism: "We've done more for veterans than any administration in history."

- **Date:** August 8, 2019
- **Situation:** Remarks on veterans' issues
- **Correct Response:** While Trump's administration implemented some policies for veterans, such as the VA MISSION Act, many of these initiatives built on previous reforms. Other administrations

also made significant contributions to veterans' services.

Trumpism: "We have the strongest military in the world, and it's getting stronger every day."

- **Date:** January 1, 2020
- **Situation:** Remarks during a New Year's Eve event
- **Correct Response:** The U.S. military is one of the most powerful globally. However, strength and readiness are constantly evolving, and comparisons with other countries, including their military advancements, show a complex global military landscape.

Trumpism: "I have never met a more dishonest person than [James Comey]."

- **Date:** April 12, 2018
- **Situation:** Remarks on former FBI Director James Comey
- **Correct Response:** James Comey's tenure and subsequent actions were controversial and subject to scrutiny, but labeling him as the "most dishonest person" was a subjective assessment and part of broader disputes over his role in the investigations.

Trumpism: "The U.S. has achieved energy independence."

- **Date:** September 18, 2020
- **Situation:** Remarks at an energy policy event
- **Correct Response:** While the U.S. significantly increased its oil production and reduced dependence on foreign oil, it is not entirely energy independent. The U.S. still imports and exports oil and natural gas, and energy markets are interconnected globally.

Trumpism: "We're winning the war on drugs."

- **Date:** October 5, 2019

- **Situation:** Remarks during a campaign rally
- **Correct Response:** The opioid crisis and other drug-related issues continued to affect many communities throughout Trump's presidency. Despite various initiatives, drug addiction and related problems persisted, making this statement overly optimistic.

Trumpism: "We've got the best military equipment. Nobody else has what we have."

- **Date:** July 16, 2019
- **Situation:** Remarks at a defense industry event
- **Correct Response:** The U.S. has advanced military technology, but other countries, including China and Russia, have also developed sophisticated military equipment. The statement exaggerated the exclusivity of U.S. military technology.

Trumpism: "We're going to bring back the coal industry."

- **Date:** March 28, 2017
- **Situation:** Remarks on energy policy
- **Correct Response:** While Trump's administration promoted policies favorable to the coal industry, such as deregulation, the coal industry continued to face challenges from market forces and competition from natural gas and renewable energy sources. The industry did not experience a significant revival.

Trumpism: "We have the greatest economy in the history of our country."

- **Date:** February 4, 2020
- **Situation:** State of the Union Address
- **Correct Response:** The U.S. economy experienced strong growth and low unemployment during Trump's presidency, but the claim of "the greatest" is debated. Economic performance varies across

historical periods, and factors like the COVID-19 pandemic impacted the economy significantly.

Trumpism: "The Wall Street Journal supports my policies."

- **Date:** June 21, 2018
- **Situation:** Remarks during a press briefing
- **Correct Response:** While some policies might have been supported by certain editorial voices, the Wall Street Journal's editorial board expressed differing opinions on various aspects of Trump's policies. The statement oversimplified the publication's stance.

Trumpism: "The economy is booming because of my tax cuts."

- **Date:** December 17, 2019
- **Situation:** Remarks on economic performance
- **Correct Response:** The Tax Cuts and Jobs Act of 2017 had some impact on economic growth, but many factors, including global economic conditions and pre-existing trends, influenced economic performance. Attributing the entire economic boom solely to tax cuts oversimplifies the broader economic context.

Trumpism: "The trade deal with Mexico is the biggest trade deal ever."

- **Date:** December 10, 2019
- **Situation:** Remarks on the USMCA
- **Correct Response:** The United States-Mexico-Canada Agreement (USMCA) updated NAFTA but was not the largest trade deal ever. Previous trade agreements, such as the Trans-Pacific Partnership (TPP), involved more countries and broader economic coverage.

Trumpism: "The press is trying to undermine the economy."

- **Date:** October 15, 2020
- **Situation:** Remarks during a campaign rally
- **Correct Response:** The media's role in reporting on the economy is to provide information and analysis. Claims that the press is deliberately trying to undermine the economy often reflect a broader criticism of media coverage rather than specific actions to harm economic performance.

Trumpism: "I've achieved the best deals for the U.S. in history."

- **Date:** August 12, 2019
- **Situation:** Remarks on trade deals
- **Correct Response:** Trade deals such as the USMCA were significant, but comparisons to historical deals depend on various factors including economic impact, negotiation terms, and long-term effects. The statement was often criticized for its lack of nuanced evaluation of trade agreements.

Trumpism: "I'm the best thing that ever happened to the African American community."

- **Date:** July 23, 2018
- **Situation:** Remarks during a press conference
- **Correct Response:** While the Trump administration implemented some policies affecting the African American community, such as criminal justice reform, many experts and advocates argue that the overall impact was mixed and that previous administrations also made significant contributions.

Trumpism: "We're seeing record-low unemployment rates across the board."

- **Date:** January 10, 2020
- **Situation:** Remarks during a State of the Union address

- **Correct Response:** Unemployment rates did reach historically low levels during Trump's presidency, but this was influenced by pre-existing trends and policies from previous administrations. Additionally, the COVID-19 pandemic led to a sharp increase in unemployment rates in 2020.

Trumpism: "The media is making up stories about the coronavirus."

- **Date:** March 17, 2020
- **Situation:** Remarks during a press briefing
- **Correct Response:** Media coverage of the coronavirus pandemic was based on scientific data and expert opinions. While there were varying reports and analyses, the pandemic itself was not fabricated, and accurate reporting was crucial for public awareness and response.

Trumpism: "We have the best economy in the history of the world."

- **Date:** October 10, 2019
- **Situation:** Remarks during a campaign rally
- **Correct Response:** The U.S. economy experienced strong growth during Trump's presidency, but claims of it being the "best in the history of the world" are debated. Economic performance is relative and varies across different historical periods and economic conditions.

Trumpism: "We've done more for farmers than any administration in history."

- **Date:** September 19, 2019
- **Situation:** Remarks during a rural economic event
- **Correct Response:** While Trump's administration implemented policies like the Trade Mitigation Program to support farmers affected by trade disputes, other administrations have also made

significant contributions to agriculture and rural communities.

Trumpism: "I have a very good relationship with Kim Jong-un."

- **Date:** June 30, 2019
- **Situation:** Remarks after a summit with North Korean leader Kim Jong-un
- **Correct Response:** The relationship between Trump and Kim Jong-un was characterized by high-level meetings and diplomatic engagement. However, the broader issues of North Korean denuclearization and human rights continued to be complex and unresolved.

Trumpism: "I'm the most pro-life president ever."

- **Date:** January 22, 2020
- **Situation:** Remarks on the anniversary of Roe v. Wade
- **Correct Response:** While Trump's administration took actions to restrict abortion access, such as reinstating the Mexico City Policy, the label of "most pro-life" is subjective. Previous presidents also took significant steps related to abortion policies.

Trumpism: "The Russia investigation was a witch hunt."

- **Date:** May 22, 2019
- **Situation:** Remarks following the release of the Mueller report
- **Correct Response:** The Mueller investigation was a legitimate and thorough inquiry into Russian interference in the 2016 election. While Trump and his allies labeled it a "witch hunt," the investigation led to numerous indictments and convictions and raised serious concerns about election security.

Trumpism: "The U.S. is the cleanest country in the world."

- **Date:** December 4, 2019
- **Situation:** Remarks at a climate change conference
- **Correct Response:** The U.S. has made progress in reducing pollution but is not the cleanest country in the world. Many countries, particularly in Europe, have lower levels of environmental pollution and have implemented more aggressive environmental policies.

Trumpism: "The U.S. has the best health care system in the world."

- **Date:** March 14, 2018
- **Situation:** Remarks on health care reform
- **Correct Response:** The U.S. health care system is advanced in many areas but faces significant issues like high costs and unequal access. Countries with universal health care systems often achieve better health outcomes and have lower costs.

Trumpism: "We're going to win so much that you're going to be amazed."

- **Date:** August 18, 2016
- **Situation:** Campaign rally
- **Correct Response:** This statement was a broad promise of success. The outcomes of various policies and achievements during Trump's presidency were mixed, and many complex issues could not be addressed simply by claiming victory.

Trumpism: "The Mueller report exonerated me completely."

- **Date:** April 18, 2019
- **Situation:** Remarks following the release of the Mueller report
- **Correct Response:** The Mueller report did not exonerate Trump completely. It did not establish criminal conspiracy but detailed numerous contacts with Russian officials and potential obstruction

of justice, leaving the matter to Congress and the public.

Trumpism: "We are cutting regulations at a record pace."

- **Date:** July 16, 2018
- **Situation:** Remarks on deregulation
- **Correct Response:** The Trump administration did roll back many regulations, particularly in environmental and business sectors. However, the term "record pace" can be debated, as previous administrations also engaged in significant regulatory changes.

Trumpism: "I'm the best dealmaker in the history of politics."

- **Date:** September 12, 2016
- **Situation:** Remarks during a campaign speech
- **Correct Response:** Trump's dealmaking skills were prominent in his business career and political negotiations. However, whether he is the "best" dealmaker is subjective and depends on evaluating the outcomes and impacts of his deals compared to historical precedents.

Trumpism: "We have the best military in the world, and we're going to make it even stronger."

- **Date:** January 8, 2020
- **Situation:** Remarks during a defense policy speech
- **Correct Response:** The U.S. military is one of the most advanced globally. However, other countries are also advancing their military capabilities, and the strength and readiness of any military are complex and subject to ongoing challenges and improvements.

Trumpism: "We've done more for the American worker than any other administration."

- **Date:** August 1, 2019
- **Situation:** Remarks on economic policy
- **Correct Response:** Various policies were aimed at benefiting American workers, but the impact is debated. Other administrations also implemented significant labor and economic reforms, and comparisons often depend on specific criteria and contexts.

Trumpism: "The stock market has never been higher."

- **Date:** January 31, 2020
- **Situation:** Remarks on the economy
- **Correct Response:** The stock market reached record highs during Trump's presidency, but this was part of a broader economic trend influenced by various factors. Historical highs in the stock market have occurred under different administrations.

Trumpism: "We have the best economy ever, and it's all because of me."

- **Date:** October 15, 2019
- **Situation:** Remarks at a campaign rally
- **Correct Response:** The U.S. economy experienced growth during Trump's presidency, but attributing it entirely to his policies oversimplifies the factors involved, including pre-existing economic conditions and global economic trends.

Trumpism: "We've made more progress on North Korea than any other administration."

- **Date:** February 28, 2019
- **Situation:** Remarks after the Hanoi summit with Kim Jong-un
- **Correct Response:** Progress on North Korea's denuclearization and relations remained limited despite high-profile summits. Subsequent actions and negotiations showed ongoing challenges,

and other administrations also worked on North Korea-related issues.

Trumpism: "The coronavirus is just like the flu."

- **Date:** February 26, 2020
- **Situation:** Press briefing on COVID-19
- **Correct Response:** COVID-19 and the flu are caused by different viruses, and COVID-19 has proven to be more contagious and severe in many cases. Comparing COVID-19 to the flu minimized the unique risks and impacts of the pandemic.

Trumpism: "I've done more for women than any president."

- **Date:** July 31, 2020
- **Situation:** Remarks on women's issues
- **Correct Response:** Trump's administration took actions related to women's issues, but previous presidents also implemented significant policies and reforms affecting women. The claim is subjective and depends on specific policy evaluations and impacts.

Trumpism: "My administration has been the most transparent in history."

- **Date:** November 15, 2019
- **Situation:** Remarks during a press conference
- **Correct Response:** Issues with transparency during Trump's administration included conflicts of interest, reluctance to release tax returns, and limited access to certain records. The claim of being "most transparent" was often disputed by critics.

Trumpism: "The military is getting the biggest pay raise in years."

- **Date:** August 1, 2018

- **Situation:** Remarks on defense policy
- **Correct Response:** While the military did receive a pay raise, it was part of a broader annual process that includes adjustments to compensation. Historical pay raises have varied, and the statement exaggerated the uniqueness of the increase.

Trumpism: "The tax cuts are paying for themselves."

- **Date:** December 20, 2018
- **Situation:** Remarks on the Tax Cuts and Jobs Act
- **Correct Response:** The claim that tax cuts would "pay for themselves" was debated. While the tax cuts did spur some economic activity, they also contributed to increased deficits and did not fully offset the revenue losses from the cuts.

Trumpism: "The FBI's investigation into Russian interference was a fraud."

- **Date:** December 12, 2019
- **Situation:** Remarks on the FBI and Russia investigation
- **Correct Response:** The FBI's investigation into Russian interference was a legitimate and thorough inquiry, although it faced criticism and controversy. The findings and actions taken during the investigation were part of broader concerns about election security.

Trumpism: "We are negotiating the greatest trade deals in history."

- **Date:** August 27, 2019
- **Situation:** Remarks on trade negotiations
- **Correct Response:** Trade deals like the USMCA were significant updates to previous agreements, but calling them the "greatest" is subjective. Historical trade deals have had varying impacts and achievements.

Trumpism: "The media is not reporting the successes of my administration."

- **Date:** March 5, 2020
- **Situation:** Remarks during a press briefing
- **Correct Response:** Media coverage often includes both successes and criticisms of any administration. The claim that successes are not reported overlooks the complex and varied nature of news coverage and reporting.

Trumpism: "My approval ratings are the highest they've ever been."

- **Date:** November 4, 2020
- **Situation:** Remarks on approval ratings
- **Correct Response:** Approval ratings fluctuated throughout Trump's presidency, with highs and lows based on various factors. Claims of the highest ratings are relative and can be influenced by specific events and timing.

Trumpism: "I was against the Iraq War from the beginning."

- **Date:** October 6, 2016
- **Situation:** Remarks during a presidential debate
- **Correct Response:** Trump's claim of being against the Iraq War from the start is disputed. While he expressed opposition in the years leading up to his presidency, he had made conflicting statements about the war and its aftermath earlier in his career.

Trumpism: "The U.S. has the highest test numbers for COVID-19 in the world, and it's a sign of our success."

- **Date:** July 23, 2020
- **Situation:** Press briefing on COVID-19 testing
- **Correct Response:** While the U.S. conducted a large number of

COVID-19 tests, high testing numbers alone do not indicate overall success. The effectiveness of testing is also dependent on timely access, accuracy, and response to the pandemic.

Trumpism: "The Democratic Party is the party of crime."

- **Date:** October 10, 2020
- **Situation:** Remarks during a campaign rally
- **Correct Response:** Labeling an entire political party as the "party of crime" oversimplifies complex issues related to crime and criminal justice. Crime rates and policies are influenced by a variety of factors, and such statements can be misleading and polarizing.

Trumpism: "We're creating the best trade deals ever."

- **Date:** June 13, 2019
- **Situation:** Remarks on trade policy
- **Correct Response:** While the Trump administration negotiated significant trade deals, such as the USMCA, the assertion of "best ever" is subjective. Trade deals have varying impacts and comparisons depend on specific terms and historical context.

Trumpism: "The economy is stronger than ever."

- **Date:** February 21, 2020
- **Situation:** Remarks on economic performance
- **Correct Response:** The U.S. economy was strong in many respects before the COVID-19 pandemic, but calling it "stronger than ever" overlooks fluctuations and the impact of global economic conditions. The pandemic significantly affected economic conditions.

Trumpism: "We've done more for small businesses than any other administration."

- **Date:** May 15, 2020
- **Situation:** Remarks on economic policy and small business support
- **Correct Response:** The Trump administration implemented policies aimed at supporting small businesses, such as the Paycheck Protection Program. However, previous administrations also enacted significant measures to aid small businesses.

Trumpism: "The U.S. has never had a better relationship with Israel."

- **Date:** January 29, 2020
- **Situation:** Remarks on U.S.-Israel relations
- **Correct Response:** The U.S.-Israel relationship has historically been strong, with various administrations fostering close ties. The Trump administration made notable moves, such as recognizing Jerusalem as Israel's capital, but the strength of the relationship is subject to historical context.

Trumpism: "We have the most secure election system in the world."

- **Date:** November 16, 2020
- **Situation:** Remarks on election integrity
- **Correct Response:** Election security is a complex issue with varying levels of vulnerability and safeguards. While the U.S. has robust systems in place, claims of being the "most secure" overlook ongoing concerns and challenges related to election integrity.

Trumpism: "The trade war with China is going very well."

- **Date:** December 31, 2018
- **Situation:** Remarks on U.S.-China trade relations
- **Correct Response:** The trade war with China led to significant economic disruptions and uncertainties for many businesses and consumers. While some agreements were reached, the overall

impact was mixed, and the situation remained complex.

Trumpism: "I'm the most self-financed candidate ever."

- **Date:** March 29, 2016
- **Situation:** Remarks during a campaign event
- **Correct Response:** While Trump did self-fund a significant portion of his 2016 campaign, he was not the first or only self-financed candidate in U.S. history. Other candidates have also funded their campaigns through personal resources.

Trumpism: "My tax cuts are going to benefit everyone."

- **Date:** December 17, 2017
- **Situation:** Remarks on the Tax Cuts and Jobs Act
- **Correct Response:** While the tax cuts aimed to benefit individuals and businesses, the actual benefits varied widely. Critics argued that the cuts disproportionately favored the wealthy and increased the national deficit.

Trumpism: "We're going to get rid of Obamacare."

- **Date:** January 20, 2017
- **Situation:** Inauguration speech
- **Correct Response:** The Trump administration made efforts to repeal and replace the Affordable Care Act (Obamacare), but full repeal did not occur. Some aspects of the law were modified or removed, but key components remained in place.

Trumpism: "We have the best military strategy in the world."

- **Date:** September 6, 2019
- **Situation:** Remarks on national security
- **Correct Response:** The U.S. military strategy is highly advanced,

but claiming it is the "best" overlooks the complexity of global military strategies and the diverse approaches taken by other nations.

Trumpism: "We have achieved peace in the Middle East."

- **Date:** August 13, 2020
- **Situation:** Announcement of the Abraham Accords
- **Correct Response:** The Abraham Accords represented a significant diplomatic achievement, establishing normalization agreements between Israel and several Arab nations. However, lasting peace in the broader Middle East remains complex and ongoing.

Trumpism: "The impeachment was a hoax."

- **Date:** December 19, 2019
- **Situation:** Remarks on impeachment proceedings
- **Correct Response:** The impeachment process was a legitimate constitutional procedure based on allegations of misconduct. While Trump and his allies characterized it as a "hoax," the impeachment involved serious legal and political considerations.

Trumpism: "We have the lowest crime rate in history."

- **Date:** July 23, 2020
- **Situation:** Remarks on crime statistics
- **Correct Response:** Crime rates fluctuate over time and can vary significantly by location. While some crime rates were low during Trump's presidency, claiming the lowest in history overlooks historical trends and regional variations.

Trumpism: "The U.S. has the strongest economy in the world."

- **Date:** September 15, 2019
- **Situation:** Remarks on economic performance
- **Correct Response:** The U.S. economy is one of the largest and most influential globally, but other economies also play significant roles in the world economy. The strength of the economy is subject to various global and domestic factors.

Trumpism: "The media is only focused on negative stories."

- **Date:** January 8, 2018
- **Situation:** Remarks during a press conference
- **Correct Response:** Media coverage includes a range of stories, both positive and negative. While criticism exists about media focus, the statement overlooks the variety of news coverage and the importance of addressing multiple aspects of current events.

Trumpism: "The border is more secure than ever."

- **Date:** February 20, 2020
- **Situation:** Remarks on border security
- **Correct Response:** Border security involves complex issues and ongoing challenges. While efforts were made to enhance security, the situation is dynamic, and issues such as illegal crossings and border management continued to be areas of concern.

Trumpism: "The economy will come roaring back after the pandemic."

- **Date:** May 1, 2020
- **Situation:** Remarks on economic recovery
- **Correct Response:** Economic recovery from the COVID-19 pandemic was uncertain and varied across sectors. While there were signs of recovery, many challenges persisted, and the pace of recovery depended on numerous factors, including public health measures and economic policies.

Trumpism: "I have the biggest crowds in history."

- **Date:** January 21, 2017
- **Situation:** Remarks about inauguration crowd sizes
- **Correct Response:** Claims about having the "biggest crowds" were disputed. Official photographs and estimates showed that the 2017 inauguration crowd was smaller compared to previous inaugurations, such as Obama's in 2009.

Trumpism: "We have rebuilt the military to be stronger than ever."

- **Date:** June 4, 2018
- **Situation:** Remarks on military spending
- **Correct Response:** The Trump administration increased military spending, but whether the military was "stronger than ever" is subjective. Military strength involves numerous factors, including readiness, technology, and strategic capabilities.

Trumpism: "The American people love me."

- **Date:** October 12, 2020
- **Situation:** Remarks during a campaign rally
- **Correct Response:** Public opinion on Trump was highly polarized, with strong support from some and significant criticism from others. The statement oversimplifies the diverse range of opinions held by the American people.

Trumpism: "We have the best trade deals ever."

- **Date:** September 9, 2019
- **Situation:** Remarks on trade agreements
- **Correct Response:** The Trump administration negotiated new trade deals like the USMCA. While these deals were significant, calling them the "best ever" is subjective and depends on

comparing them with historical trade agreements.

Trumpism: "We've done more to fight corruption than any previous administration."

- **Date:** April 25, 2019
- **Situation:** Remarks on anti-corruption efforts
- **Correct Response:** Anti-corruption efforts during Trump's presidency included various initiatives, but previous administrations also took significant steps to address corruption. Comparing effectiveness involves examining various policies and actions.

Trumpism: "We're seeing record job creation."

- **Date:** February 1, 2019
- **Situation:** Remarks on job growth
- **Correct Response:** Job creation during Trump's presidency was strong, but "record" job creation is relative to historical trends. Job growth is influenced by various factors, including economic conditions and policies from previous administrations.

Trumpism: "The U.S. has the highest standard of living in the world."

- **Date:** August 17, 2019
- **Situation:** Remarks on quality of life
- **Correct Response:** The U.S. has a high standard of living but is not the only country with a high quality of life. Different countries excel in various aspects such as health care, education, and overall well-being.

Trumpism: "My administration has the lowest staff turnover in history."

- **Date:** October 22, 2019

- **Situation:** Remarks on staff stability
- **Correct Response:** The Trump administration experienced significant staff turnover compared to other administrations. High turnover rates were noted throughout his presidency, contrasting with the claim of "lowest" turnover.

Trumpism: "The economy was the best it's ever been before the pandemic."

- **Date:** June 15, 2020
- **Situation:** Remarks on pre-pandemic economic conditions
- **Correct Response:** The economy was strong before the pandemic, but calling it the "best ever" overlooks historical economic performance and fluctuations over time. Various economic indicators and historical periods can offer different perspectives.

Trumpism: "I'm the only president to get a trade deal with China."

- **Date:** January 15, 2020
- **Situation:** Remarks on trade negotiations
- **Correct Response:** Previous administrations also negotiated trade agreements with China. The Phase One trade deal signed during Trump's presidency was a significant development, but not the only trade agreement with China.

Trumpism: "I have done more for the military than any president in history."

- **Date:** November 10, 2019
- **Situation:** Remarks on military achievements
- **Correct Response:** The Trump administration increased military spending and made changes in defense policy, but whether he did "more" than any other president is subjective and depends on evaluating a range of military and defense policies over time.

Trumpism: "The U.S. has the highest COVID-19 testing rate in the world."

- **Date:** April 17, 2020
- **Situation:** Remarks on COVID-19 testing
- **Correct Response:** The U.S. did have a high number of COVID-19 tests conducted, but testing rates need to be considered relative to the population and other countries' testing efforts. High testing rates alone do not fully measure a country's response to the pandemic.

Trumpism: "I am the least racist person you will ever meet."

- **Date:** July 19, 2019
- **Situation:** Remarks during a press conference
- **Correct Response:** This statement was made in response to accusations of racism. While Trump denied being racist, many of his statements and actions were criticized as racially insensitive or discriminatory by various groups and individuals.

Trumpism: "We've done more to lower drug prices than any other administration."

- **Date:** May 11, 2020
- **Situation:** Remarks on health care policy
- **Correct Response:** The Trump administration made efforts to address drug pricing, but whether it achieved more than previous administrations is debated. The complexity of drug pricing involves various factors, including legislation and market dynamics.

Trumpism: "The media never covers the great things we do."

- **Date:** August 15, 2020
- **Situation:** Remarks on media coverage

- **Correct Response:** Media coverage includes a wide range of topics, including both achievements and criticisms. Claims that only negative stories are covered overlook the diversity of news reporting and the challenges of media representation.

Trumpism: "I have the best health care plan ever."

- **Date:** July 26, 2017
- **Situation:** Remarks on health care reform
- **Correct Response:** The Trump administration proposed changes to health care but did not pass a comprehensive replacement for the Affordable Care Act. The effectiveness and quality of any health care plan are subject to analysis and comparison with existing plans.

Trumpism: "The economy was booming before the pandemic hit."

- **Date:** April 1, 2020
- **Situation:** Remarks on economic conditions
- **Correct Response:** The U.S. economy was performing well before the pandemic, with low unemployment and growth. However, the term "booming" is subjective and does not account for ongoing economic issues and disparities.

Trumpism: "I am the most successful businessman to ever become president."

- **Date:** December 20, 2017
- **Situation:** Remarks on business success
- **Correct Response:** Trump's business career was notable, but claiming he is the "most successful" is subjective and depends on evaluating the achievements of other businessman-presidents, such as Herbert Hoover and Jimmy Carter.

Trumpism: "The wall is almost complete."

- **Date:** February 11, 2020
- **Situation:** Remarks on border security
- **Correct Response:** The Trump administration made progress on border barriers, but the wall was not fully completed by the end of his term. Various sections were rebuilt or replaced, but the project did not achieve the original scope.

Trumpism: "I have accomplished more in my first term than any other president."

- **Date:** October 2, 2020
- **Situation:** Remarks during a campaign rally
- **Correct Response:** The Trump administration had notable achievements and challenges, but whether it accomplished "more" than any other president is subjective and involves comparing various accomplishments across different administrations.

Trumpism: "I've created the best job numbers in history."

- **Date:** July 24, 2020
- **Situation:** Remarks on employment statistics
- **Correct Response:** Job creation was strong during Trump's presidency, but "best numbers" depend on historical context and specific metrics. Economic conditions and job growth are influenced by a range of factors beyond the presidency.

Trumpism: "The media is trying to rig the election."

- **Date:** October 22, 2020
- **Situation:** Remarks on election integrity
- **Correct Response:** Allegations of media bias and interference are often debated. While media coverage can influence public

perception, the integrity of elections involves numerous factors, including voting processes and regulations.

Trumpism: "My administration has the most successful foreign policy."

- **Date:** September 30, 2020
- **Situation:** Remarks on international relations
- **Correct Response:** The Trump administration's foreign policy had significant impacts, but success is subjective and depends on evaluating outcomes in various regions and issues. Different administrations have pursued diverse foreign policy strategies.

Trumpism: "We have the best response to COVID-19 in the world."

- **Date:** August 23, 2020
- **Situation:** Remarks on the U.S. COVID-19 response
- **Correct Response:** While the U.S. implemented various measures to address COVID-19, other countries had different strategies and outcomes. The effectiveness of the response is subject to analysis and comparison with global efforts.

Trumpism: "We have the most transparent administration ever."

- **Date:** June 12, 2019
- **Situation:** Remarks on government transparency
- **Correct Response:** The Trump administration faced criticism regarding transparency, including conflicts of interest and access to information. Claims of being the "most transparent" contrast with criticisms from various watchdog groups.

Trumpism: "My tax plan is the biggest tax cut in history."

- **Date:** November 27, 2017
- **Situation:** Remarks on tax reform

- **Correct Response:** The Tax Cuts and Jobs Act was significant, but whether it was the "biggest" in history depends on how one measures tax cuts and compares them with past reforms and their impact on different income groups.

Trumpism: "The unemployment rate is the lowest it's ever been."

- **Date:** October 5, 2020
- **Situation:** Remarks on unemployment statistics
- **Correct Response:** Unemployment rates were low prior to the COVID-19 pandemic, but not historically the lowest ever. Unemployment rates fluctuated over time, and the pandemic caused a significant increase in unemployment.

Trumpism: "We've defeated ISIS."

- **Date:** October 23, 2019
- **Situation:** Remarks on ISIS and Middle East policy
- **Correct Response:** The territorial defeat of ISIS was a significant achievement, but the group's influence and activities continued in various forms. The situation in the Middle East remained complex with ongoing challenges.

Trumpism: "I'm the most popular president in history."

- **Date:** March 17, 2020
- **Situation:** Remarks on presidential popularity
- **Correct Response:** Popularity is measured by various metrics, including approval ratings and election results. Trump's approval ratings fluctuated and were often polarized, making claims of being the "most popular" subjective.

Trumpism: "I'm the best negotiator ever."

- **Date:** September 19, 2018
- **Situation:** Remarks on negotiation skills
- **Correct Response:** Negotiation skills are subjective and can be evaluated in different contexts. Trump's negotiation tactics were both praised and criticized, and claims of being the "best" depend on individual perspectives and outcomes.

Trumpism: "We have the safest border ever."

- **Date:** October 2, 2019
- **Situation:** Remarks on border security
- **Correct Response:** The U.S. made various efforts to enhance border security, but calling it the "safest ever" oversimplifies ongoing challenges and the complexities of border management and security.

Trumpism: "I'm the greatest president for the economy."

- **Date:** January 30, 2020
- **Situation:** Remarks on economic achievements
- **Correct Response:** Economic performance is influenced by many factors and historical context. Claims of being the "greatest" president for the economy are subjective and involve comparing achievements with those of other administrations.

Trumpism: "The media is spreading fake news about my administration."

- **Date:** May 14, 2018
- **Situation:** Remarks on media coverage
- **Correct Response:** The term "fake news" has been used to describe various media reports. While some reports may be inaccurate, media coverage includes a wide range of stories and perspectives, and the accuracy of reporting varies.

Trumpism: "The trade deal with Mexico and Canada is the best ever."

- **Date:** November 30, 2018
- **Situation:** Remarks on the USMCA trade agreement
- **Correct Response:** The USMCA updated the North American Free Trade Agreement (NAFTA). While the deal had significant changes, claiming it is the "best ever" is subjective and depends on evaluating its impact compared to other trade agreements.

Trumpism: "I've done more for farmers than any other president."

- **Date:** October 15, 2019
- **Situation:** Remarks on agricultural policy
- **Correct Response:** The Trump administration implemented policies affecting agriculture, but whether it did "more" for farmers than any other president involves evaluating various agricultural policies and their impacts historically.

Trumpism: "I have the most incredible relationship with North Korea."

- **Date:** June 30, 2019
- **Situation:** Remarks following a summit with North Korea
- **Correct Response:** Trump's relationship with North Korea was notable for high-profile summits and diplomacy. However, the overall situation with North Korea remains complex, with ongoing challenges related to denuclearization and regional security.

Trumpism: "The wall is almost finished, and it's beautiful."

- **Date:** February 12, 2020
- **Situation:** Remarks on border wall progress
- **Correct Response:** The border wall was not completed by the end of Trump's term. While some barriers were constructed or replaced, the project did not achieve its original scope and faced

significant logistical and financial challenges.

Trumpism: "I'm the best president for the economy in modern history."

- **Date:** August 23, 2020
- **Situation:** Remarks on economic performance
- **Correct Response:** The Trump administration saw strong economic performance before the COVID-19 pandemic, but the claim of being the "best president for the economy" is subjective and depends on comparing various economic indicators and historical contexts.

Trumpism: "We've eliminated the regulatory burden like never before."

- **Date:** July 16, 2019
- **Situation:** Remarks on deregulation efforts
- **Correct Response:** The Trump administration rolled back numerous regulations, but whether this was "like never before" depends on historical comparisons. Previous administrations also implemented deregulation efforts in various sectors.

Trumpism: "The Democrats are trying to steal the election."

- **Date:** November 5, 2020
- **Situation:** Remarks on election integrity
- **Correct Response:** Claims of election theft were widely investigated, with no evidence of widespread fraud that would have affected the outcome. Such statements can undermine trust in the electoral process and are subject to verification and legal review.

Trumpism: "I've done more for African Americans than any other president."

- **Date:** February 20, 2020

- **Situation:** Remarks on achievements for African Americans
- **Correct Response:** The Trump administration implemented policies aimed at benefiting African Americans, but claims of having done "more" than any other president are subjective and depend on evaluating historical achievements across administrations.

Trumpism: "We have the best health care system in the world."

- **Date:** March 24, 2020
- **Situation:** Remarks on health care
- **Correct Response:** The U.S. health care system is highly advanced but faces significant challenges, including accessibility and costs. The claim of having the "best" system is subjective and depends on comparing it with other countries' health care systems.

Trumpism: "I've achieved the lowest unemployment rate for women."

- **Date:** September 8, 2020
- **Situation:** Remarks on employment statistics
- **Correct Response:** Unemployment rates for women were low before the COVID-19 pandemic, but the claim of being the "lowest" depends on comparing historical data. The pandemic had a significant impact on employment statistics.

Trumpism: "I'm bringing back American manufacturing like never before."

- **Date:** April 30, 2019
- **Situation:** Remarks on manufacturing policy
- **Correct Response:** The Trump administration focused on promoting American manufacturing, but whether this was "like never before" involves evaluating manufacturing trends and comparing them with historical data.

Trumpism: "We have the best record on veterans' care."

- **Date:** November 11, 2019
- **Situation:** Remarks on veterans' services
- **Correct Response:** The Trump administration made efforts to improve veterans' care, but the "best record" is subjective and depends on comparing it with the achievements and challenges faced by previous administrations.

Trumpism: "We have rebuilt the military like no one else."

- **Date:** May 23, 2019
- **Situation:** Remarks on defense spending
- **Correct Response:** The Trump administration increased defense spending, but comparing it to previous administrations involves evaluating various defense strategies and historical contexts. Claims of "rebuilding like no one else" are subjective.

Trumpism: "The trade deals I've made are the best deals ever."

- **Date:** January 16, 2020
- **Situation:** Remarks on trade agreements
- **Correct Response:** The Trump administration negotiated several significant trade deals, but whether they are the "best" deals depends on evaluating their impact compared to other historical trade agreements and their outcomes.

Trumpism: "The media is always lying about my administration."

- **Date:** November 7, 2018
- **Situation:** Remarks on media coverage
- **Correct Response:** Media coverage includes a variety of stories, some of which may be critical. Claims of "always lying" do not account for the range of coverage and differing perspectives in

journalism.

Trumpism: "We have the lowest immigration levels in decades."

- **Date:** July 28, 2019
- **Situation:** Remarks on immigration policy
- **Correct Response:** Immigration levels fluctuate due to various factors. While the Trump administration implemented policies that reduced certain types of immigration, historical data shows varying trends over decades.

Trumpism: "I have the most successful foreign policy achievements of any president."

- **Date:** August 25, 2020
- **Situation:** Remarks on foreign policy
- **Correct Response:** Trump's foreign policy included notable achievements, but calling them the "most successful" depends on comparing them with the foreign policy achievements of other presidents across different contexts and issues.

Trumpism: "I've created more jobs than any president in history."

- **Date:** September 10, 2020
- **Situation:** Remarks on job creation
- **Correct Response:** Job creation was a focus during Trump's presidency, but whether he created more jobs than any other president involves evaluating historical job growth data and economic conditions.

Trumpism: "The U.S. has the best trade relationships ever."

- **Date:** March 21, 2019
- **Situation:** Remarks on trade relations

- **Correct Response:** The U.S. engaged in various trade negotiations and agreements, but whether trade relationships are the "best ever" depends on comparing them with historical trade relations and their outcomes.

Trumpism: "I've done more for small businesses than any other president."

- **Date:** April 4, 2020
- **Situation:** Remarks on small business policies
- **Correct Response:** The Trump administration implemented policies aimed at supporting small businesses, but claims of doing "more" than any other president are subjective and depend on evaluating historical support for small businesses.

Trumpism: "The economy is the best it's ever been."

- **Date:** December 11, 2019
- **Situation:** Remarks on economic performance
- **Correct Response:** Economic conditions were strong before the pandemic, but calling it the "best ever" is subjective and depends on historical comparisons of economic performance across different periods.

Trumpism: "I've created the most jobs for veterans."

- **Date:** July 24, 2020
- **Situation:** Remarks on job creation for veterans
- **Correct Response:** The Trump administration took steps to support veterans' employment, but whether it created the "most" jobs for veterans involves evaluating historical data and comparing it with efforts by other administrations.

Trumpism: "The COVID-19 vaccine was developed in record time thanks to my administration."

- **Date:** December 8, 2020
- **Situation:** Remarks on vaccine development
- **Correct Response:** The COVID-19 vaccines were developed quickly due to collaborative efforts including Operation Warp Speed, which was supported by the Trump administration, but also involved extensive work from pharmaceutical companies and researchers.

Trumpism: "I have the most significant achievements in foreign policy since World War II."

- **Date:** February 4, 2020
- **Situation:** Remarks on foreign policy achievements
- **Correct Response:** The Trump administration's foreign policy included various initiatives, but calling them the "most significant" since World War II depends on comparing them with historical foreign policy achievements and their global impact.

Trumpism: "We have the most advanced military technology ever."

- **Date:** May 22, 2019
- **Situation:** Remarks on military technology
- **Correct Response:** The U.S. has advanced military technology, but claims of having the "most advanced" depend on comparing it with other countries' technological advancements and developments in defense systems.

Trumpism: "I have the best record on economic growth."

- **Date:** January 15, 2020
- **Situation:** Remarks on economic growth

- **Correct Response:** Economic growth was strong before the pandemic, but the claim of having the "best record" involves comparing growth rates and economic conditions with other periods and administrations.

Trumpism: "I'm responsible for the lowest crime rates in history."

- **Date:** June 25, 2020
- **Situation:** Remarks on crime rates
- **Correct Response:** Crime rates fluctuate due to various factors. The Trump administration focused on law enforcement, but the lowest crime rates in history are subject to historical data and comparisons with previous periods.

Trumpism: "I've done more to support law enforcement than any other president."

- **Date:** July 27, 2020
- **Situation:** Remarks on support for law enforcement
- **Correct Response:** The Trump administration supported law enforcement through various policies, but comparing this support to previous presidents involves evaluating different approaches and outcomes in law enforcement support.

Trumpism: "I have the best plan for health care in history."

- **Date:** October 2, 2020
- **Situation:** Remarks on health care plans
- **Correct Response:** The Trump administration proposed changes to health care, but whether it is the "best plan" is subjective and involves evaluating the effectiveness of proposed plans compared to existing ones.

Trumpism: "We've achieved the lowest tax rates for businesses."

- **Date:** December 22, 2019
- **Situation:** Remarks on business tax rates
- **Correct Response:** The Tax Cuts and Jobs Act lowered business tax rates, but claims of achieving the "lowest" rates depend on comparing them with historical tax rates and other reforms over time.

Trumpism: "My administration has created the strongest military in the world."

- **Date:** September 18, 2020
- **Situation:** Remarks on military strength
- **Correct Response:** The U.S. military is a major global power, but claims of being the "strongest" involve comparing military capabilities with other nations and evaluating various aspects of military strength and readiness.

Trumpism: "We have the most robust economy in history."

- **Date:** November 10, 2019
- **Situation:** Remarks on economic conditions
- **Correct Response:** The U.S. economy was strong before the pandemic, but the claim of being the "most robust" involves comparing current economic conditions with historical data and performance across different periods.

Trumpism: "We have the most successful trade deals ever."

- **Date:** January 29, 2020
- **Situation:** Remarks on trade agreements
- **Correct Response:** The Trump administration renegotiated trade deals like USMCA, but whether they are the "most successful" depends on comparing their impacts and outcomes with previous trade agreements.

Trumpism: "My administration has done more to protect religious freedom than any other."

- **Date:** October 27, 2020
- **Situation:** Remarks on religious freedom
- **Correct Response:** The Trump administration made changes affecting religious freedom, but claims of doing "more" depend on evaluating historical efforts and policies regarding religious rights and protections.

Trumpism: "We've cut more regulations than any other administration."

- **Date:** February 10, 2020
- **Situation:** Remarks on deregulation
- **Correct Response:** The Trump administration rolled back numerous regulations, but the extent of these cuts compared to previous administrations involves evaluating regulatory changes and their impacts across different sectors.

Trumpism: "The border is more secure than ever before."

- **Date:** March 15, 2020
- **Situation:** Remarks on border security
- **Correct Response:** The Trump administration implemented various border security measures, but the claim of being "more secure" is subjective and involves assessing ongoing challenges and improvements in border management.

Trumpism: "I have the most effective economic policies."

- **Date:** September 30, 2020
- **Situation:** Remarks on economic policy effectiveness
- **Correct Response:** The effectiveness of economic policies is subject to analysis and comparison with policies from other

administrations. Claims of being "most effective" depend on evaluating various economic indicators and outcomes.

Trumpism: "I've done more for trade than any president before me."

- **Date:** July 1, 2020
- **Situation:** Remarks on trade achievements
- **Correct Response:** The Trump administration negotiated significant trade deals, but comparing these achievements to those of previous presidents involves evaluating their impact on trade relations and economic outcomes.

Trumpism: "My administration has the best record on job creation."

- **Date:** October 20, 2020
- **Situation:** Remarks on job creation
- **Correct Response:** Job creation was strong before the COVID-19 pandemic, but whether it was the "best record" depends on comparing job growth data with that of other administrations across different economic conditions.

Trumpism: "The media never covers the great economy we had before the pandemic."

- **Date:** July 12, 2020
- **Situation:** Remarks on media coverage of the economy
- **Correct Response:** Media coverage includes various aspects of the economy, both positive and negative. Claims of only focusing on negative aspects overlook the range of economic reporting and the context of media coverage.

Trumpism: "We have the lowest crime rates in history thanks to my policies."

- **Date:** November 4, 2020
- **Situation:** Remarks on crime reduction
- **Correct Response:** Crime rates fluctuate due to numerous factors. While some policies may impact crime, calling them the "lowest in history" involves evaluating trends and comparing them with historical data across different periods.

Trumpism: "I've accomplished the most for American workers."

- **Date:** August 1, 2020
- **Situation:** Remarks on accomplishments for workers
- **Correct Response:** The Trump administration implemented policies aimed at benefiting American workers, but claims of accomplishing the "most" involve comparing these efforts with those of previous administrations and their impacts.

Trumpism: "My tax cuts are the biggest in history."

- **Date:** December 12, 2017
- **Situation:** Remarks on tax cuts
- **Correct Response:** The Tax Cuts and Jobs Act represented a significant tax cut, but whether it is the "biggest" in history depends on comparing it with other major tax reforms and their impacts on different income groups.

Trumpism: "I've made the best deals for America's farmers."

- **Date:** September 18, 2020
- **Situation:** Remarks on agricultural policies
- **Correct Response:** The Trump administration took steps to support farmers, but claims of making the "best deals" involve evaluating these policies in comparison to historical support for agriculture and their effectiveness.

Trumpism: "We have the strongest national security ever."

- **Date:** March 12, 2020
- **Situation:** Remarks on national security
- **Correct Response:** National security involves numerous factors, and the strength of national security is subject to evaluation and comparison with previous administrations' approaches and outcomes.

Trumpism: "The U.S. has never been in better shape economically."

- **Date:** August 15, 2020
- **Situation:** Remarks on economic conditions
- **Correct Response:** Economic conditions were strong before the COVID-19 pandemic, but claims of being in the "best shape" depend on comparing economic performance across different historical periods and contexts.

Trumpism: "My administration has had the most transparent response to COVID-19."

- **Date:** April 14, 2020
- **Situation:** Remarks on COVID-19 response transparency
- **Correct Response:** The Trump administration's response to COVID-19 was subject to criticism regarding transparency and communication. Evaluations of transparency involve assessing the availability and clarity of information provided to the public.

Trumpism: "We've achieved the highest GDP growth in decades."

- **Date:** February 12, 2020
- **Situation:** Remarks on GDP growth
- **Correct Response:** The U.S. experienced strong GDP growth prior to the pandemic, but whether it was the highest in decades

depends on comparing growth rates with historical data and economic conditions over time.

Trumpism: "I'm the best president for veterans in history."

- **Date:** November 11, 2019
- **Situation:** Remarks on support for veterans
- **Correct Response:** The Trump administration made efforts to support veterans, but whether it was the "best" for veterans involves comparing these efforts with those of previous administrations and evaluating their impacts.

Trumpism: "My trade policies are making America great again."

- **Date:** August 10, 2019
- **Situation:** Remarks on trade policy impacts
- **Correct Response:** The impacts of trade policies are complex and involve various factors, including trade balances and relationships. Evaluating whether they are making "America great again" depends on analyzing their overall effects on the economy and trade relationships.

Trumpism: "I've done more to cut taxes for the middle class than any other president."

- **Date:** December 15, 2019
- **Situation:** Remarks on tax cuts for the middle class
- **Correct Response:** The Tax Cuts and Jobs Act included provisions for the middle class, but whether it is "more" than other presidents' efforts depends on comparing the impacts of various tax reforms over time.

Trumpism: "We have the best health care system in the world thanks to my policies."

- **Date:** October 1, 2020
- **Situation:** Remarks on health care system
- **Correct Response:** The U.S. health care system has advanced in many ways, but calling it the "best" depends on comparing it with health care systems in other countries and evaluating different aspects of care and access.

Trumpism: "I've reduced the national debt more than any other president."

- **Date:** March 3, 2020
- **Situation:** Remarks on national debt reduction
- **Correct Response:** The national debt increased during the Trump administration due to various factors, including spending and tax cuts. Claims of reducing the debt "more" than other presidents are not accurate in this context.

Trumpism: "The economy was the strongest it's ever been before the pandemic."

- **Date:** June 30, 2020
- **Situation:** Remarks on pre-pandemic economic strength
- **Correct Response:** The U.S. economy was strong before the pandemic, but comparing it to other periods involves evaluating historical economic data and considering different economic conditions over time.

Trumpism: "We've made the biggest investment in the military in history."

- **Date:** November 15, 2019
- **Situation:** Remarks on military investment
- **Correct Response:** The Trump administration increased military spending, but whether it is the "biggest" investment involves

comparing it with historical defense budgets and expenditures over time.

Trumpism: "My administration has the most secure border ever."

- **Date:** January 22, 2020
- **Situation:** Remarks on border security
- **Correct Response:** Border security measures were enhanced, but the claim of being the "most secure" involves evaluating ongoing challenges and improvements in border management compared to previous periods.

Trumpism: "The media is always unfair to my administration."

- **Date:** February 25, 2019
- **Situation:** Remarks on media coverage
- **Correct Response:** Media coverage includes a range of perspectives and stories. Claims of being "always unfair" do not account for the diversity of coverage and different viewpoints in journalism.

Trumpism: "We have the best trade relations with China ever."

- **Date:** June 18, 2020
- **Situation:** Remarks on trade relations with China
- **Correct Response:** Trade relations with China involved significant negotiations and changes. Whether they are the "best ever" depends on evaluating trade balances and agreements compared to previous relations.

Trumpism: "My administration has the most effective foreign policy achievements."

- **Date:** August 8, 2020

- **Situation:** Remarks on foreign policy achievements
- **Correct Response:** The Trump administration's foreign policy included various initiatives, but evaluating them as the "most effective" involves comparing them with the achievements of other administrations and their global impact.

Trumpism: "I've done more for the American economy than any president before me."

- **Date:** November 5, 2019
- **Situation:** Remarks on economic performance
- **Correct Response:** The Trump administration implemented various economic policies, but claiming to have done "more" than any other president involves comparing these policies and outcomes with those of previous administrations.

Trumpism: "We have the strongest job market in history."

- **Date:** December 12, 2019
- **Situation:** Remarks on job market strength
- **Correct Response:** The job market was strong before the COVID-19 pandemic, but claims of being the "strongest in history" involve evaluating job market data and conditions across different historical periods.

Trumpism: "I've reduced the number of regulations more than any other administration."

- **Date:** February 25, 2020
- **Situation:** Remarks on deregulation
- **Correct Response:** The Trump administration rolled back numerous regulations, but comparing this to previous administrations involves evaluating the scope and impact of regulatory changes over time.

Trumpism: "My administration has done the most for farmers in history."

- **Date:** October 15, 2020
- **Situation:** Remarks on support for farmers
- **Correct Response:** The Trump administration supported farmers through various programs, but whether it did the "most" involves comparing these efforts with historical support and policies for agriculture.

Trumpism: "The United States has never been more respected globally."

- **Date:** August 10, 2020
- **Situation:** Remarks on global respect
- **Correct Response:** Global respect for the U.S. is influenced by various factors, including foreign policy and international relations. Evaluating whether it has "never been more respected" involves assessing global perceptions and diplomatic relationships.

Trumpism: "I've achieved the lowest illegal immigration rates in decades."

- **Date:** March 22, 2020
- **Situation:** Remarks on illegal immigration
- **Correct Response:** The Trump administration took steps to reduce illegal immigration, but claims of achieving the "lowest" rates involve comparing current data with historical immigration trends.

Trumpism: "My trade war with China has been an overwhelming success."

- **Date:** December 30, 2019
- **Situation:** Remarks on trade policy with China

- **Correct Response:** The trade war with China had significant economic impacts and mixed results. Evaluating it as an "overwhelming success" depends on analyzing the overall effects on trade balances and economic outcomes.

Trumpism: "The media never talks about the success of my policies."

- **Date:** January 25, 2020
- **Situation:** Remarks on media coverage of policies
- **Correct Response:** Media coverage includes a range of stories, including both successes and criticisms. Claims of only focusing on failures do not account for the diversity of reporting and the range of policy impacts covered.

Trumpism: "I've made the biggest improvements to the VA system."

- **Date:** July 27, 2020
- **Situation:** Remarks on Veterans Affairs improvements
- **Correct Response:** The Trump administration made changes to the VA system, but whether these improvements are the "biggest" involves comparing them with reforms and changes made by previous administrations.

Trumpism: "My economic policies have resulted in the fastest economic growth ever."

- **Date:** September 15, 2020
- **Situation:** Remarks on economic growth
- **Correct Response:** Economic growth was strong before the pandemic, but comparing it to previous periods involves evaluating growth rates and economic conditions over different historical contexts.

Trumpism: "I have the best record on crime reduction."

- **Date:** August 30, 2020
- **Situation:** Remarks on crime reduction
- **Correct Response:** Crime rates can be influenced by numerous factors. Evaluating the "best record" on crime reduction involves comparing crime data and policy impacts with those of previous administrations.

Trumpism: "The U.S. has the most secure elections in history."

- **Date:** October 1, 2020
- **Situation:** Remarks on election security
- **Correct Response:** Election security involves various factors and ongoing efforts to address potential vulnerabilities. Claims of being the "most secure" involve assessing election integrity measures compared to historical standards and practices.

Trumpism: "My administration has achieved the best results in national security."

- **Date:** September 12, 2020
- **Situation:** Remarks on national security achievements
- **Correct Response:** National security outcomes involve multiple factors and assessments. Evaluating the "best results" involves comparing national security policies and achievements with those of previous administrations.

Trumpism: "We've achieved the lowest tax rates in history for individuals."

- **Date:** December 22, 2019
- **Situation:** Remarks on individual tax rates
- **Correct Response:** The Tax Cuts and Jobs Act lowered individual tax rates, but comparing these rates to historical standards involves analyzing the impact of tax reforms and their effects on different

income groups over time.

Trumpism: "I've created the best economy ever for working families."

- **Date:** August 5, 2019
- **Situation:** Remarks on economic benefits for working families
- **Correct Response:** The Trump administration implemented policies affecting working families, but whether it created the "best" economy involves comparing these benefits with those of previous administrations and assessing overall economic conditions.

Trumpism: "My administration has the most robust foreign policy in history."

- **Date:** November 1, 2020
- **Situation:** Remarks on foreign policy strength
- **Correct Response:** The Trump administration's foreign policy included various strategies and initiatives. Evaluating it as the "most robust" involves comparing these efforts with historical foreign policy approaches and outcomes.

Trumpism: "We have the lowest crime rates in urban areas ever."

- **Date:** March 5, 2020
- **Situation:** Remarks on crime rates in urban areas
- **Correct Response:** Crime rates in urban areas fluctuate due to various factors. The claim of being the "lowest ever" depends on comparing current data with historical crime statistics and analyzing trends over time.

Trumpism: "I've done more for American manufacturing than any other president."

- **Date:** October 25, 2020
- **Situation:** Remarks on support for manufacturing
- **Correct Response:** The Trump administration took steps to support American manufacturing, but comparing these efforts to those of previous presidents involves evaluating the impact of manufacturing policies and their results.

Trumpism: "We have the best job creation numbers in history."

- **Date:** January 12, 2020
- **Situation:** Remarks on job creation
- **Correct Response:** Job creation numbers were strong before the pandemic, but whether they are the "best in history" involves comparing job growth data with that of previous periods and different economic contexts.

Trumpism: "My administration has achieved unprecedented success in reducing the trade deficit."

- **Date:** July 15, 2020
- **Situation:** Remarks on trade deficit reduction
- **Correct Response:** The trade deficit is influenced by various factors, including trade policies. Evaluating the "unprecedented success" in reducing it involves comparing changes in the trade deficit with historical data and other administrations' results.

Trumpism: "We've secured the most comprehensive health care reforms ever."

- **Date:** September 30, 2019
- **Situation:** Remarks on health care reforms
- **Correct Response:** The Trump administration proposed and enacted changes to health care, but whether they are the "most comprehensive" involves assessing these reforms compared to past

health care legislation and reforms.

Trumpism: "I've made the biggest strides in reducing illegal immigration."

- **Date:** June 20, 2020
- **Situation:** Remarks on illegal immigration reduction
- **Correct Response:** The Trump administration took measures to address illegal immigration, but evaluating the "biggest strides" involves comparing current immigration data with historical trends and the impact of various policies.

Trumpism: "My economic policies have produced the greatest wealth creation ever."

- **Date:** April 10, 2020
- **Situation:** Remarks on economic wealth creation
- **Correct Response:** Economic wealth creation is influenced by numerous factors, including policy decisions. Claims of "greatest wealth creation" involve comparing economic outcomes and wealth distribution with historical data.

Trumpism: "The U.S. has never been stronger on national security."

- **Date:** October 10, 2020
- **Situation:** Remarks on national security strength
- **Correct Response:** National security strength involves various measures and assessments. Evaluating whether the U.S. has "never been stronger" involves comparing current national security conditions with those of previous periods.

Trumpism: "My administration's tax cuts are the most beneficial for small businesses."

- **Date:** August 12, 2020
- **Situation:** Remarks on tax cuts for small businesses
- **Correct Response:** The Tax Cuts and Jobs Act included provisions for small businesses, but whether they are the "most beneficial" involves comparing these cuts with those from previous policies and their impacts on small businesses.

Trumpism: "I've done more to support the military than any other president."

- **Date:** July 4, 2020
- **Situation:** Remarks on support for the military
- **Correct Response:** The Trump administration increased military spending and support, but whether it did "more" than any other president involves comparing military support efforts and outcomes with those of previous administrations.

Trumpism: "My administration has achieved the highest level of energy independence."

- **Date:** February 24, 2020
- **Situation:** Remarks on energy independence
- **Correct Response:** The U.S. made progress toward energy independence, but evaluating it as the "highest level" involves comparing current energy production and consumption with historical data and policies.

Trumpism: "We have the most successful economic recovery in history."

- **Date:** November 8, 2020
- **Situation:** Remarks on economic recovery
- **Correct Response:** Economic recovery involves analyzing various factors and timelines. Comparing it to previous recoveries involves evaluating the speed and effectiveness of recovery efforts across

different economic conditions.

Trumpism: "My administration has provided the largest tax relief ever."

- **Date:** December 16, 2019
- **Situation:** Remarks on tax relief
- **Correct Response:** The Tax Cuts and Jobs Act provided significant tax relief, but whether it is the "largest ever" depends on comparing it with historical tax relief measures and their impacts.

Trumpism: "We have the most comprehensive immigration reform ever."

- **Date:** October 5, 2020
- **Situation:** Remarks on immigration reform
- **Correct Response:** The Trump administration implemented various immigration policies, but calling it the "most comprehensive" involves comparing these reforms with past immigration legislation and their impacts.

Trumpism: "I've delivered the best trade agreements in history."

- **Date:** July 8, 2020
- **Situation:** Remarks on trade agreements
- **Correct Response:** The Trump administration negotiated trade agreements like USMCA, but evaluating them as the "best in history" involves comparing these agreements with previous trade deals and their outcomes.

Trumpism: "My administration has made the greatest strides in criminal justice reform."

- **Date:** September 20, 2020
- **Situation:** Remarks on criminal justice reform

- **Correct Response:** The Trump administration enacted some criminal justice reforms, but whether they represent the "greatest strides" involves comparing these efforts with historical reforms and their impacts on the justice system.

Trumpism: "We have achieved unprecedented levels of job creation."

- **Date:** June 5, 2020
- **Situation:** Remarks on job creation
- **Correct Response:** Job creation was strong before the pandemic, but comparing it to other periods involves evaluating job growth rates and economic conditions over different historical contexts.

Trumpism: "My administration has delivered the strongest border security ever."

- **Date:** August 1, 2020
- **Situation:** Remarks on border security
- **Correct Response:** The Trump administration took measures to enhance border security, but whether it is the "strongest ever" involves evaluating these measures in comparison to previous border security efforts and challenges.

Trumpism: "I've made the best deals for American workers."

- **Date:** July 22, 2019
- **Situation:** Remarks on deals benefiting American workers
- **Correct Response:** The Trump administration negotiated various policies affecting workers, but assessing whether they are the "best deals" involves comparing these outcomes with those of previous administrations.

Trumpism: "We have the most effective health care policies in history."

- **Date:** October 15, 2019
- **Situation:** Remarks on health care policies
- **Correct Response:** Health care policies have evolved over time. Evaluating them as the "most effective" involves comparing current policies with past reforms and their impacts on health care access and quality.

Trumpism: "I've achieved the lowest unemployment rate in history."

- **Date:** September 4, 2019
- **Situation:** Remarks on unemployment rates
- **Correct Response:** Unemployment rates were low before the COVID-19 pandemic, but comparing them to historical lows involves evaluating unemployment data across different periods and economic conditions.

Trumpism: "My administration has set new records in economic growth."

- **Date:** December 20, 2019
- **Situation:** Remarks on economic growth
- **Correct Response:** Economic growth was strong before the pandemic, but whether it set new records involves comparing growth rates with historical data and other periods of economic expansion.

Trumpism: "We have the most successful foreign policy ever."

- **Date:** August 30, 2020
- **Situation:** Remarks on foreign policy success
- **Correct Response:** Success in foreign policy involves various aspects and outcomes. Evaluating it as the "most successful" involves comparing current policies and achievements with those of previous administrations.

Trumpism: "I've done more for the economy than any president in history."

- **Date:** July 15, 2020
- **Situation:** Remarks on economic achievements
- **Correct Response:** The Trump administration made significant economic changes, but claiming to have done "more" involves comparing these achievements with those of previous presidents and evaluating their overall economic impact.

Trumpism: "My administration has achieved the highest level of energy production."

- **Date:** October 10, 2019
- **Situation:** Remarks on energy production
- **Correct Response:** U.S. energy production increased during the Trump administration, but evaluating it as the "highest level" involves comparing current production levels with historical data and trends in energy production.

Trumpism: "We have the strongest economy in the world."

- **Date:** September 25, 2020
- **Situation:** Remarks on global economic strength
- **Correct Response:** The U.S. economy was strong before the pandemic, but whether it is the "strongest" involves comparing it with other major economies and considering various economic indicators and global economic conditions.

Trumpism: "My administration has achieved the lowest poverty rates in decades."

- **Date:** September 28, 2020
- **Situation:** Remarks on poverty rates

- **Correct Response:** Poverty rates were affected by various factors, including economic conditions and policy changes. Evaluating them as the "lowest in decades" involves comparing current rates with historical data and considering different socioeconomic contexts.

Trumpism: "We have the best record on deregulation in history."

- **Date:** March 15, 2020
- **Situation:** Remarks on deregulation
- **Correct Response:** The Trump administration rolled back many regulations, but whether it is the "best record" involves comparing these deregulation efforts with those of previous administrations and evaluating their impacts.

Trumpism: "I've made the largest investments in infrastructure in history."

- **Date:** August 14, 2020
- **Situation:** Remarks on infrastructure investment
- **Correct Response:** The Trump administration proposed infrastructure plans, but whether they represent the "largest investments" involves comparing these plans with historical infrastructure spending and their impacts.

Trumpism: "My administration has achieved the highest level of job satisfaction."

- **Date:** October 8, 2019
- **Situation:** Remarks on job satisfaction
- **Correct Response:** Job satisfaction is influenced by various factors and surveys. Evaluating it as the "highest level" involves comparing job satisfaction metrics with historical data and considering different economic and employment conditions.

Trumpism: "We have the most successful economic policies for small businesses ever."

- **Date:** December 22, 2019
- **Situation:** Remarks on economic policies for small businesses
- **Correct Response:** The Trump administration implemented policies affecting small businesses, but whether they are the "most successful" involves comparing these policies with those of previous administrations and their impacts on small businesses.

Trumpism: "I've done more to enhance veterans' benefits than any other president."

- **Date:** November 11, 2019
- **Situation:** Remarks on veterans' benefits
- **Correct Response:** The Trump administration made changes to veterans' benefits, but comparing these changes with those from previous administrations involves evaluating the scope and impact of various veterans' programs and reforms.

Trumpism: "My administration has achieved unprecedented success in reducing national debt."

- **Date:** May 15, 2020
- **Situation:** Remarks on national debt reduction
- **Correct Response:** The national debt increased during the Trump administration due to spending and tax cuts. Evaluating claims of "unprecedented success" involves comparing national debt trends with historical data and the effects of fiscal policies.

Trumpism: "We have the most effective policies for economic recovery."

- **Date:** August 1, 2020
- **Situation:** Remarks on economic recovery policies

- **Correct Response:** Economic recovery policies involve various measures and contexts. Evaluating them as the "most effective" involves comparing recovery efforts and outcomes with those of previous periods and different economic conditions.

Trumpism: "I've achieved the best results in reducing crime rates."

- **Date:** June 10, 2020
- **Situation:** Remarks on crime reduction
- **Correct Response:** Crime rates are influenced by multiple factors, and evaluating the "best results" involves comparing crime data and policy impacts with those of previous administrations and different historical contexts.

Trumpism: "My administration has delivered the strongest support for the manufacturing sector."

- **Date:** July 18, 2020
- **Situation:** Remarks on support for manufacturing
- **Correct Response:** The Trump administration implemented policies affecting manufacturing, but evaluating it as the "strongest support" involves comparing these efforts with historical support for the manufacturing sector and their impacts.

Trumpism: "We have the most secure borders in history."

- **Date:** September 5, 2020
- **Situation:** Remarks on border security
- **Correct Response:** Border security involves various measures and challenges. Evaluating it as the "most secure" involves comparing current border security conditions with historical data and previous security measures.

Trumpism: "My administration's tax cuts have been the most beneficial for the economy."

- **Date:** January 10, 2020
- **Situation:** Remarks on the impact of tax cuts
- **Correct Response:** The Tax Cuts and Jobs Act impacted the economy, but whether it was the "most beneficial" involves comparing these tax cuts with those from previous administrations and analyzing their overall economic effects.

Trumpism: "We have achieved the best trade balance ever."

- **Date:** October 20, 2020
- **Situation:** Remarks on trade balance
- **Correct Response:** The trade balance is influenced by numerous factors, including trade policies and global economic conditions. Evaluating it as the "best ever" involves comparing current trade balances with historical data and trade policies.

Trumpism: "I've done more to support rural communities than any other president."

- **Date:** August 25, 2020
- **Situation:** Remarks on support for rural communities
- **Correct Response:** The Trump administration implemented policies affecting rural communities, but comparing these efforts to those of previous presidents involves evaluating the scope and impact of rural development initiatives.

Trumpism: "My administration has the most effective foreign trade policies."

- **Date:** November 12, 2020
- **Situation:** Remarks on foreign trade policies

- **Correct Response:** Foreign trade policies involve various agreements and strategies. Evaluating them as the "most effective" involves comparing these policies with historical trade agreements and their impacts on global trade relationships.

Trumpism: "My administration's economic growth is the best in modern history."

- **Date:** June 20, 2019
- **Situation:** Remarks on economic growth
- **Correct Response:** Economic growth during the Trump administration was notable, but evaluating it as the "best in modern history" involves comparing growth rates and economic conditions with those of other recent administrations.

Trumpism: "We've achieved record-low unemployment for minorities."

- **Date:** December 6, 2019
- **Situation:** Remarks on unemployment rates among minorities
- **Correct Response:** Unemployment rates among minorities reached record lows before the pandemic, but comparing these rates with historical data involves evaluating trends and impacts over time.

Trumpism: "My administration's border policies are the toughest ever."

- **Date:** July 22, 2020
- **Situation:** Remarks on border policy enforcement
- **Correct Response:** The Trump administration enforced strict border policies, but whether they are the "toughest ever" involves comparing these policies with historical enforcement measures and their effectiveness.

Trumpism: "My tax cuts have led to the greatest economic expansion."

- **Date:** February 15, 2020
- **Situation:** Remarks on economic expansion due to tax cuts
- **Correct Response:** Tax cuts can impact economic expansion, but evaluating them as leading to the "greatest expansion" involves analyzing economic growth data and comparing it to previous periods of expansion.

Trumpism: "We have the strongest job market for veterans ever."

- **Date:** October 12, 2020
- **Situation:** Remarks on job market conditions for veterans
- **Correct Response:** Job market conditions for veterans improved during the Trump administration, but evaluating it as the "strongest ever" involves comparing these conditions with historical data and support measures for veterans.

Trumpism: "My administration has done more to reduce the national debt than any other."

- **Date:** August 14, 2020
- **Situation:** Remarks on national debt reduction
- **Correct Response:** The national debt increased during the Trump administration, so comparing the reduction efforts with historical data involves evaluating debt trends and the impacts of fiscal policies.

Trumpism: "We've achieved the most effective trade agreements for American workers."

- **Date:** November 4, 2020
- **Situation:** Remarks on trade agreements
- **Correct Response:** Trade agreements like USMCA were negotiated, but whether they are the "most effective" involves comparing these agreements with past trade deals and their

impacts on American workers.

Trumpism: "My administration's deregulation efforts have been the most impactful."

- **Date:** March 10, 2020
- **Situation:** Remarks on deregulation impacts
- **Correct Response:** The Trump administration rolled back many regulations, but assessing their impact involves comparing these efforts with those of previous administrations and their overall effects.

Trumpism: "We have the best results in infrastructure development."

- **Date:** July 28, 2020
- **Situation:** Remarks on infrastructure development
- **Correct Response:** Infrastructure development was a focus, but whether it resulted in the "best results" involves comparing these developments with past infrastructure projects and their effectiveness.

Trumpism: "My administration has achieved the highest levels of energy independence."

- **Date:** September 18, 2020
- **Situation:** Remarks on energy independence
- **Correct Response:** Energy independence was a goal, and the U.S. made progress, but evaluating it as the "highest level" involves comparing current energy independence with historical production and consumption data.

Trumpism: "We have the strongest national security policies ever."

- **Date:** August 24, 2020

- **Situation:** Remarks on national security policies
- **Correct Response:** National security policies include various strategies and measures. Evaluating them as the "strongest ever" involves comparing these policies with those of previous administrations and their effectiveness.

Trumpism: "My administration's health care reforms are the most comprehensive."

- **Date:** October 30, 2019
- **Situation:** Remarks on health care reforms
- **Correct Response:** The Trump administration proposed changes to health care, but evaluating them as the "most comprehensive" involves comparing these reforms with past health care legislation and their impacts.

Trumpism: "I've delivered the highest job growth rates for women."

- **Date:** July 6, 2020
- **Situation:** Remarks on job growth for women
- **Correct Response:** Job growth for women improved during the Trump administration, but comparing it to other periods involves evaluating job growth rates and conditions for women over time.

Trumpism: "We have the most successful policies for rural development."

- **Date:** September 22, 2020
- **Situation:** Remarks on rural development policies
- **Correct Response:** Rural development policies were implemented, but evaluating them as the "most successful" involves comparing these policies with historical rural development efforts and their impacts.

Trumpism: "My administration has achieved the best trade deals for American farmers."

- **Date:** October 16, 2020
- **Situation:** Remarks on trade deals affecting farmers
- **Correct Response:** Trade deals like USMCA included provisions for agriculture, but evaluating them as the "best" involves comparing these deals with previous trade agreements and their effects on farmers.

Trumpism: "We've made the greatest progress in reducing corporate tax rates."

- **Date:** December 11, 2019
- **Situation:** Remarks on corporate tax rate changes
- **Correct Response:** The Tax Cuts and Jobs Act lowered corporate tax rates, but whether it represents the "greatest progress" involves comparing these changes with past tax reforms and their impacts on businesses.

Trumpism: "I've delivered the most significant military funding increases."

- **Date:** July 10, 2020
- **Situation:** Remarks on military funding
- **Correct Response:** The Trump administration increased military spending, but assessing it as "most significant" involves comparing these funding increases with those of previous administrations and their effects on military capabilities.

Trumpism: "We have the lowest rates of illegal immigration in decades."

- **Date:** August 5, 2020
- **Situation:** Remarks on illegal immigration rates

- **Correct Response:** Illegal immigration rates fluctuated during the Trump administration, but evaluating them as the "lowest in decades" involves comparing current rates with historical data and considering the impact of various policies.

Trumpism: "My administration's environmental policies are the most effective ever."

- **Date:** September 10, 2020
- **Situation:** Remarks on environmental policies
- **Correct Response:** The Trump administration rolled back several environmental regulations, and evaluating them as the "most effective" involves comparing these policies with past environmental efforts and their overall impact on the environment.

Trumpism: "We've achieved unprecedented levels of infrastructure investment."

- **Date:** October 25, 2020
- **Situation:** Remarks on infrastructure investment
- **Correct Response:** The Trump administration proposed infrastructure plans, but assessing them as "unprecedented" involves comparing these investments with historical infrastructure spending and their outcomes.

Trumpism: "I've done more to support American energy independence than any other president."

- **Date:** November 2, 2020
- **Situation:** Remarks on energy independence support
- **Correct Response:** The U.S. made strides in energy independence during the Trump administration, but evaluating it as "more" than other presidents involves comparing energy policies and production levels over time.

Trumpism: "My administration has achieved the most successful deregulation in history."

- **Date:** June 15, 2020
- **Situation:** Remarks on deregulation success
- **Correct Response:** The Trump administration undertook significant deregulation efforts, but whether they are the "most successful" involves comparing these efforts with past deregulation measures and their impacts.

Trumpism: "We have the highest levels of job creation for minorities ever."

- **Date:** August 22, 2020
- **Situation:** Remarks on job creation for minorities
- **Correct Response:** Job creation for minorities improved, but evaluating it as the "highest levels ever" involves comparing job growth rates and conditions for minorities with historical data.

Trumpism: "My administration has achieved the best results in combating human trafficking."

- **Date:** December 30, 2019
- **Situation:** Remarks on efforts to combat human trafficking
- **Correct Response:** Efforts to combat human trafficking were part of various policies, but evaluating them as the "best results" involves comparing these efforts with historical data and effectiveness of previous administrations' policies.

Trumpism: "We've made the greatest strides in criminal justice reform."

- **Date:** July 20, 2020
- **Situation:** Remarks on criminal justice reform
- **Correct Response:** The Trump administration enacted the First

Step Act, among other measures, but evaluating them as the "greatest strides" involves comparing these reforms with past criminal justice efforts and their impacts.

Trumpism: "I've provided the most robust support for American innovation."

- **Date:** September 12, 2020
- **Situation:** Remarks on support for innovation
- **Correct Response:** The Trump administration supported various innovation initiatives, but evaluating it as "most robust" involves comparing these efforts with previous administrations' support for innovation and technological advancement.

Trumpism: "My administration has achieved record-low rates of foreign aid."

- **Date:** October 8, 2020
- **Situation:** Remarks on foreign aid levels
- **Correct Response:** Foreign aid levels were adjusted during the Trump administration, but evaluating them as "record-low" involves comparing current levels with historical data and considering changes in foreign policy priorities.

Trumpism: "We've achieved the best results in improving national infrastructure."

- **Date:** July 30, 2020
- **Situation:** Remarks on infrastructure improvements
- **Correct Response:** Infrastructure improvements were a focus of the Trump administration, but assessing them as the "best results" involves comparing these improvements with those of previous periods and their overall effectiveness.

Trumpism: "My administration has delivered the highest standards of fiscal responsibility."

- **Date:** November 7, 2020
- **Situation:** Remarks on fiscal responsibility
- **Correct Response:** Fiscal responsibility involves managing spending and deficits. Evaluating it as the "highest standards" involves comparing these efforts with historical fiscal management and budgetary outcomes.

Trumpism: "We've achieved the lowest rates of crime in American history."

- **Date:** August 17, 2020
- **Situation:** Remarks on crime rates
- **Correct Response:** Crime rates fluctuated during the Trump administration, and while some crime rates were lower, evaluating them as "the lowest in history" involves comparing these rates with historical data and trends over different periods.

Trumpism: "My administration's immigration policies are the most humane ever."

- **Date:** October 5, 2020
- **Situation:** Remarks on immigration policies
- **Correct Response:** Immigration policies under Trump were controversial, with critics arguing they were inhumane. Evaluating them as "most humane" involves comparing these policies with those of previous administrations and their treatment of immigrants.

Trumpism: "We've achieved record high levels of job satisfaction."

- **Date:** December 20, 2020

- **Situation:** Remarks on job satisfaction
- **Correct Response:** Job satisfaction is influenced by various factors and surveys. Evaluating it as "record high" involves comparing job satisfaction metrics with historical data and overall economic conditions.

Trumpism: "My administration's trade policies are the most beneficial for American workers."

- **Date:** September 8, 2020
- **Situation:** Remarks on trade policies
- **Correct Response:** The Trump administration's trade policies, including tariffs and renegotiated agreements, aimed to benefit American workers, but evaluating them as "most beneficial" involves comparing these policies with past trade policies and their impacts.

Trumpism: "We've made the greatest improvements in veterans' health care."

- **Date:** July 25, 2020
- **Situation:** Remarks on veterans' health care
- **Correct Response:** Improvements in veterans' health care were made, but whether they are the "greatest" involves comparing these changes with past reforms and evaluating their impacts on veterans' health care services.

Trumpism: "My administration has the most effective job creation strategies."

- **Date:** August 15, 2020
- **Situation:** Remarks on job creation strategies
- **Correct Response:** The Trump administration implemented various strategies to boost job creation, but evaluating them as

"most effective" involves comparing these strategies with those of previous administrations and their overall impact on employment.

Trumpism: "We have the strongest economic recovery ever."

- **Date:** October 1, 2020
- **Situation:** Remarks on economic recovery
- **Correct Response:** Economic recovery was ongoing during the Trump administration, but evaluating it as the "strongest ever" involves comparing recovery metrics and conditions with historical recoveries and economic performance.

Trumpism: "My administration has delivered the best results in national security."

- **Date:** November 3, 2020
- **Situation:** Remarks on national security
- **Correct Response:** National security measures were a focus of the Trump administration, but assessing them as the "best results" involves comparing these measures with past national security efforts and their effectiveness.

Trumpism: "We've achieved unprecedented levels of business deregulation."

- **Date:** July 30, 2020
- **Situation:** Remarks on deregulation
- **Correct Response:** The Trump administration undertook significant deregulation efforts, but evaluating them as "unprecedented" involves comparing these efforts with previous deregulation measures and their impacts on businesses.

Trumpism: "My administration has achieved the highest level of infrastructure development."

- **Date:** August 18, 2020
- **Situation:** Remarks on infrastructure development
- **Correct Response:** Infrastructure development efforts were a priority, but evaluating them as the "highest level" involves comparing these efforts with historical infrastructure projects and their effectiveness.

Trumpism: "We have the best record in reducing the federal deficit."

- **Date:** September 15, 2020
- **Situation:** Remarks on the federal deficit
- **Correct Response:** The federal deficit increased during the Trump administration, so evaluating it as the "best record" involves comparing deficit levels and fiscal policies with those of previous administrations.

Trumpism: "My administration's foreign policies are the most effective ever."

- **Date:** November 12, 2020
- **Situation:** Remarks on foreign policies
- **Correct Response:** Foreign policies were a significant focus, but evaluating them as the "most effective" involves comparing current foreign policy outcomes with those of past administrations and their global impacts.

Trumpism: "We've achieved the most significant tax reform in history."

- **Date:** December 15, 2019
- **Situation:** Remarks on tax reform
- **Correct Response:** The Tax Cuts and Jobs Act was a major tax reform, but whether it is the "most significant" involves comparing it with past tax reforms and their impacts on various sectors of the economy.

Trumpism: "My administration has made the most progress in combating opioid addiction."

- **Date:** October 30, 2020
- **Situation:** Remarks on combating opioid addiction
- **Correct Response:** Efforts to address opioid addiction were part of the administration's agenda, but evaluating them as "most progress" involves comparing these efforts with those of previous administrations and their impacts on the opioid crisis.

Trumpism: "We've achieved the highest levels of energy production ever."

- **Date:** August 20, 2020
- **Situation:** Remarks on energy production
- **Correct Response:** Energy production increased during the Trump administration, but assessing it as the "highest levels ever" involves comparing current production data with historical records and energy production trends.

Trumpism: "My administration has delivered the best results in reducing government waste."

- **Date:** July 5, 2020
- **Situation:** Remarks on reducing government waste
- **Correct Response:** Efforts were made to address government waste, but evaluating them as the "best results" involves comparing these efforts with past measures to reduce waste and their effectiveness.

Trumpism: "My administration has achieved the highest levels of American competitiveness."

- **Date:** September 25, 2020

- **Situation:** Remarks on American competitiveness
- **Correct Response:** American competitiveness involves various economic and trade factors. Evaluating it as the "highest levels" requires comparing competitiveness metrics with historical data and previous administrations' efforts.

Trumpism: "We've made the most progress in reducing prescription drug prices."

- **Date:** October 10, 2020
- **Situation:** Remarks on prescription drug prices
- **Correct Response:** Efforts were made to address prescription drug prices, but evaluating them as the "most progress" involves comparing these changes with past efforts and their impacts on drug pricing.

Trumpism: "My administration has the best track record in protecting religious freedoms."

- **Date:** November 5, 2020
- **Situation:** Remarks on religious freedoms
- **Correct Response:** The Trump administration made changes to policies affecting religious freedoms, but evaluating it as the "best track record" involves comparing these policies with those of previous administrations and their impacts on religious freedoms.

Trumpism: "We have the most effective policies for reducing carbon emissions."

- **Date:** August 30, 2020
- **Situation:** Remarks on carbon emissions policies
- **Correct Response:** The Trump administration rolled back several environmental regulations, so evaluating policies as "most effective" involves comparing them with past measures and their

overall impact on carbon emissions.

Trumpism: "We've achieved record high levels of economic equality."

- **Date:** December 1, 2020
- **Situation:** Remarks on economic equality
- **Correct Response:** Economic equality involves various measures and metrics. Evaluating it as "record high" involves comparing current levels with historical data and trends over time.

Trumpism: "My administration has done more to support small businesses than any other."

- **Date:** October 20, 2020
- **Situation:** Remarks on support for small businesses
- **Correct Response:** Support for small businesses was a priority, but evaluating it as "more" than any other administration involves comparing policies and support measures with those from previous administrations and their impacts.

Trumpism: "We've achieved the lowest levels of poverty in American history."

- **Date:** September 22, 2020
- **Situation:** Remarks on poverty levels
- **Correct Response:** Poverty levels fluctuated during the Trump administration. Evaluating them as "lowest in history" involves comparing current poverty rates with historical data and socioeconomic conditions.

Trumpism: "My administration has achieved the most successful tax cuts for middle-class families."

- **Date:** November 1, 2020

- **Situation:** Remarks on tax cuts for the middle class
- **Correct Response:** The Tax Cuts and Jobs Act included provisions for middle-class families, but assessing it as "most successful" involves comparing these tax cuts with past reforms and their impact on middle-class families.

Trumpism: "We have the best results in enhancing American infrastructure."

- **Date:** October 12, 2020
- **Situation:** Remarks on infrastructure enhancement
- **Correct Response:** Infrastructure enhancement was a focus, but evaluating it as the "best results" involves comparing these efforts with historical infrastructure projects and their overall effectiveness.

Trumpism: "My administration has the most effective approach to handling the trade deficit."

- **Date:** September 30, 2020
- **Situation:** Remarks on trade deficit management
- **Correct Response:** Trade deficit management involved various policies. Evaluating it as "most effective" requires comparing current trade deficits and policies with those of previous administrations and their impacts.

Trumpism: "We've achieved the highest levels of job creation for women in history."

- **Date:** August 8, 2020
- **Situation:** Remarks on job creation for women
- **Correct Response:** Job creation for women improved, but evaluating it as "highest levels" involves comparing job growth rates and employment conditions for women with historical data.

TRUMPISMS: DECODING THE RHETORIC OF DISRUPTION 101

Trumpism: "My administration has made the greatest advancements in public safety."

- **Date:** November 15, 2020
- **Situation:** Remarks on public safety advancements
- **Correct Response:** Public safety advancements were part of the administration's agenda, but assessing them as "greatest advancements" involves comparing these efforts with past public safety measures and their effectiveness.

Trumpism: "We have the most robust national economic strategy ever."

- **Date:** September 14, 2020
- **Situation:** Remarks on national economic strategy
- **Correct Response:** The Trump administration's economic strategy included various policies, but evaluating it as "most robust" involves comparing these strategies with past economic plans and their overall effectiveness.

Trumpism: "My administration has achieved unprecedented success in reducing government regulation."

- **Date:** October 25, 2020
- **Situation:** Remarks on reducing government regulation
- **Correct Response:** The Trump administration focused on deregulation, but assessing it as "unprecedented success" involves comparing these deregulation efforts with historical regulatory measures and their impacts.

Trumpism: "We've made the most significant progress in improving veterans' benefits."

- **Date:** July 15, 2020
- **Situation:** Remarks on veterans' benefits improvements

- **Correct Response:** Improvements to veterans' benefits were implemented, but evaluating them as "most significant" involves comparing these changes with past reforms and their impacts on veterans.

Trumpism: "My administration has delivered the best results in fighting terrorism."

- **Date:** September 22, 2020
- **Situation:** Remarks on counter-terrorism efforts
- **Correct Response:** The Trump administration implemented various counter-terrorism measures, but evaluating them as "best results" involves comparing these efforts with past strategies and their effectiveness in reducing terrorism.

Trumpism: "We've achieved unprecedented levels of economic growth for rural areas."

- **Date:** October 7, 2020
- **Situation:** Remarks on economic growth in rural areas
- **Correct Response:** Economic growth in rural areas was a focus, but assessing it as "unprecedented" involves comparing growth metrics with historical data and previous rural development efforts.

Trumpism: "My administration's immigration policies are the most successful in history."

- **Date:** November 4, 2020
- **Situation:** Remarks on immigration policy success
- **Correct Response:** Immigration policies were a key issue, but evaluating them as "most successful" involves comparing current policies with those of previous administrations and their overall impacts on immigration and border control.

Trumpism: "We've made the greatest strides in public health safety."

- **Date:** August 12, 2020
- **Situation:** Remarks on public health safety measures
- **Correct Response:** Public health safety was a priority, but evaluating it as "greatest strides" involves comparing these measures with those of previous administrations and their effectiveness in improving public health.

Trumpism: "My administration has the most effective strategies for reducing federal spending."

- **Date:** October 16, 2020
- **Situation:** Remarks on federal spending strategies
- **Correct Response:** Strategies to reduce federal spending were implemented, but evaluating them as "most effective" involves comparing these strategies with historical data on federal spending and their impact on the budget deficit.

Trumpism: "We've achieved the highest levels of innovation in technology."

- **Date:** September 20, 2020
- **Situation:** Remarks on technological innovation
- **Correct Response:** Technological innovation was promoted, but assessing it as "highest levels" involves comparing innovation metrics with those of previous periods and overall advancements in technology.

Trumpism: "My administration has delivered the most effective foreign aid programs."

- **Date:** November 10, 2020
- **Situation:** Remarks on foreign aid effectiveness

- **Correct Response:** Foreign aid programs were adjusted, but evaluating them as "most effective" involves comparing these programs with past foreign aid initiatives and their overall impact on recipient countries.

Trumpism: "We've achieved the lowest levels of unemployment in decades."

- **Date:** August 25, 2020
- **Situation:** Remarks on unemployment levels
- **Correct Response:** Unemployment rates varied during the Trump administration, and while they reached historically low levels before the pandemic, evaluating them as "lowest in decades" involves comparing these rates with historical data.

Trumpism: "My administration has made the greatest progress in improving education."

- **Date:** October 22, 2020
- **Situation:** Remarks on education improvements
- **Correct Response:** Education policies were implemented, but evaluating them as "greatest progress" involves comparing these efforts with past educational reforms and their impacts on education quality and access.

Trumpism: "We've achieved the most significant advances in space exploration."

- **Date:** September 18, 2020
- **Situation:** Remarks on space exploration advancements
- **Correct Response:** Space exploration efforts continued, but assessing them as "most significant" involves comparing these advancements with historical space exploration achievements and missions.

Trumpism: "My administration's trade policies are the most successful for American workers."

- **Date:** November 2, 2020
- **Situation:** Remarks on trade policy success
- **Correct Response:** Trade policies aimed to benefit American workers, but evaluating them as "most successful" involves comparing these policies with past trade agreements and their impacts on American jobs.

Trumpism: "We've made the most progress in reducing national debt."

- **Date:** July 12, 2020
- **Situation:** Remarks on national debt reduction
- **Correct Response:** The national debt increased during the Trump administration, so evaluating efforts to reduce it as "most progress" involves comparing national debt levels and fiscal policies with those of previous administrations.

Trumpism: "My administration has achieved the highest standards in cybersecurity."

- **Date:** October 29, 2020
- **Situation:** Remarks on cybersecurity standards
- **Correct Response:** Cybersecurity measures were enhanced, but evaluating them as "highest standards" involves comparing these standards with those of previous administrations and their effectiveness in protecting against cyber threats.

Trumpism: "We've achieved record-breaking results in energy efficiency."

- **Date:** August 8, 2020
- **Situation:** Remarks on energy efficiency

- **Correct Response:** Energy efficiency measures were part of the agenda, but assessing them as "record-breaking" involves comparing these results with historical energy efficiency improvements and overall impacts.

Trumpism: "My administration has done more to support working families than any other."

- **Date:** September 30, 2020
- **Situation:** Remarks on support for working families
- **Correct Response:** Support for working families was a priority, but evaluating it as "more" than any other administration involves comparing support measures and policies with those of previous administrations and their impact on working families.

Trumpism: "My administration has achieved the best results in improving American manufacturing."

- **Date:** September 15, 2020
- **Situation:** Remarks on manufacturing improvements
- **Correct Response:** American manufacturing saw some growth, but evaluating it as the "best results" involves comparing these outcomes with historical data and previous manufacturing policies.

Trumpism: "We've delivered the most comprehensive reforms to the healthcare system."

- **Date:** October 3, 2020
- **Situation:** Remarks on healthcare system reforms
- **Correct Response:** Healthcare reforms were proposed, but assessing them as "most comprehensive" involves comparing these reforms with past healthcare policies and their impacts on the healthcare system.

Trumpism: "My administration's environmental policies have resulted in the cleanest air and water in history."

- **Date:** July 10, 2020
- **Situation:** Remarks on environmental quality
- **Correct Response:** Environmental regulations were adjusted, but evaluating air and water quality as "cleanest in history" involves comparing current data with historical environmental quality metrics.

Trumpism: "We've achieved the highest levels of infrastructure investment in decades."

- **Date:** October 20, 2020
- **Situation:** Remarks on infrastructure investment
- **Correct Response:** Infrastructure investments were made, but evaluating them as the "highest levels" involves comparing these investments with historical data on infrastructure spending and development.

Trumpism: "My administration has the most effective policies for combating domestic violence."

- **Date:** August 12, 2020
- **Situation:** Remarks on domestic violence policies
- **Correct Response:** Efforts to address domestic violence were part of the administration's agenda, but evaluating them as "most effective" involves comparing these policies with past measures and their impacts.

Trumpism: "We've made the most significant advancements in rural broadband access."

- **Date:** September 25, 2020

- **Situation:** Remarks on broadband access
- **Correct Response:** Rural broadband access was improved, but assessing it as "most significant" involves comparing these advancements with past efforts and their impact on broadband availability in rural areas.

Trumpism: "My administration has achieved record high levels of small business growth."

- **Date:** October 15, 2020
- **Situation:** Remarks on small business growth
- **Correct Response:** Small business growth was a focus, but evaluating it as "record high levels" involves comparing growth metrics with historical data and previous small business policies.

Trumpism: "We've delivered the most successful public-private partnerships ever."

- **Date:** November 1, 2020
- **Situation:** Remarks on public-private partnerships
- **Correct Response:** Public-private partnerships were promoted, but evaluating them as "most successful" involves comparing these partnerships with past initiatives and their effectiveness in achieving goals.

Trumpism: "My administration has done more to improve worker wages than any other."

- **Date:** September 5, 2020
- **Situation:** Remarks on wage improvements
- **Correct Response:** Efforts to improve worker wages were part of the administration's policies, but evaluating them as "more" than any other administration involves comparing wage growth with historical data and previous wage policies.

Trumpism: "We've achieved the most significant reductions in federal bureaucracy."

- **Date:** August 18, 2020
- **Situation:** Remarks on reducing federal bureaucracy
- **Correct Response:** Reductions in federal bureaucracy were part of the administration's agenda, but assessing them as "most significant" involves comparing these reductions with past efforts and their impact on government operations.

Trumpism: "My administration's trade deals have created unprecedented opportunities for American workers."

- **Date:** October 22, 2020
- **Situation:** Remarks on trade deals
- **Correct Response:** Trade deals were negotiated, but evaluating them as creating "unprecedented opportunities" involves comparing the outcomes of these deals with past agreements and their impact on American workers.

Trumpism: "We've made the most significant progress in improving financial regulations."

- **Date:** September 10, 2020
- **Situation:** Remarks on financial regulations
- **Correct Response:** Financial regulations were adjusted, but evaluating them as "most significant" involves comparing these changes with past financial regulations and their impacts on the financial industry.

Trumpism: "My administration has achieved record-breaking results in job creation for veterans."

- **Date:** October 8, 2020

- **Situation:** Remarks on job creation for veterans
- **Correct Response:** Job creation efforts for veterans were implemented, but evaluating them as "record-breaking" involves comparing job growth metrics for veterans with historical data and previous efforts.

Trumpism: "We've achieved the highest levels of investment in scientific research."

- **Date:** August 25, 2020
- **Situation:** Remarks on scientific research investment
- **Correct Response:** Investment in scientific research was a priority, but assessing it as "highest levels" involves comparing current investment levels with historical data and previous research funding.

Trumpism: "My administration's economic policies have resulted in the most prosperous economy ever."

- **Date:** November 5, 2020
- **Situation:** Remarks on economic prosperity
- **Correct Response:** The economy experienced growth and challenges, but evaluating it as "most prosperous" involves comparing economic metrics and conditions with historical economic performance.

Trumpism: "We've delivered the most effective policies for supporting the elderly."

- **Date:** September 12, 2020
- **Situation:** Remarks on policies supporting the elderly
- **Correct Response:** Policies supporting the elderly were implemented, but evaluating them as "most effective" involves comparing these policies with past measures and their impact on

senior citizens.

Trumpism: "My administration has achieved the best results in improving national infrastructure."

- **Date:** September 30, 2020
- **Situation:** Remarks on infrastructure improvements
- **Correct Response:** Infrastructure improvements were made, but evaluating them as "best results" involves comparing these outcomes with past infrastructure projects and their overall effectiveness.

Trumpism: "We've achieved the most significant reductions in healthcare costs."

- **Date:** October 14, 2020
- **Situation:** Remarks on reducing healthcare costs
- **Correct Response:** Efforts were made to address healthcare costs, but assessing them as "most significant" involves comparing cost reductions with historical data and past healthcare policies.

Trumpism: "My administration has delivered record-breaking results in educational achievement."

- **Date:** August 22, 2020
- **Situation:** Remarks on educational achievements
- **Correct Response:** Educational achievements were a focus, but evaluating them as "record-breaking" involves comparing educational metrics and performance with historical data and previous education policies.

Trumpism: "We've made the most progress in addressing income inequality."

- **Date:** November 3, 2020
- **Situation:** Remarks on income inequality
- **Correct Response:** Addressing income inequality was part of the administration's agenda, but evaluating it as "most progress" involves comparing these efforts with past measures and their impacts on income distribution.

Trumpism: "My administration's policies have created unprecedented economic opportunities."

- **Date:** September 20, 2020
- **Situation:** Remarks on economic opportunities
- **Correct Response:** Economic policies were designed to create opportunities, but assessing them as "unprecedented" involves comparing these policies with past economic strategies and their outcomes.

Trumpism: "We've achieved the highest levels of investment in green energy."

- **Date:** October 25, 2020
- **Situation:** Remarks on green energy investment
- **Correct Response:** Investment in green energy was made, but evaluating it as "highest levels" involves comparing current investments with historical data and previous green energy initiatives.

Trumpism: "My administration has the most effective strategies for enhancing national security."

- **Date:** August 30, 2020
- **Situation:** Remarks on national security strategies
- **Correct Response:** National security strategies were implemented, but evaluating them as "most effective" involves comparing these

strategies with those of previous administrations and their overall impact on national security.

Trumpism: "My administration has achieved record-breaking reductions in federal regulations."

- **Date:** October 10, 2020
- **Situation:** Remarks on reducing federal regulations
- **Correct Response:** Federal regulations were reduced, but evaluating these reductions as "record-breaking" involves comparing them with historical data and previous deregulation efforts.

Trumpism: "We've achieved unprecedented levels of support for the agricultural sector."

- **Date:** September 7, 2020
- **Situation:** Remarks on support for agriculture
- **Correct Response:** Support for agriculture was provided, but evaluating it as "unprecedented levels" involves comparing these efforts with past agricultural policies and their impacts on the sector.

Trumpism: "My administration's criminal justice reforms are the most comprehensive ever."

- **Date:** August 15, 2020
- **Situation:** Remarks on criminal justice reforms
- **Correct Response:** Criminal justice reforms were enacted, but assessing them as "most comprehensive" involves comparing these reforms with past initiatives and their impacts on the justice system.

Trumpism: "We've achieved the best results in supporting American innovation."

- **Date:** October 18, 2020
- **Situation:** Remarks on supporting innovation
- **Correct Response:** Support for innovation was a focus, but evaluating it as "best results" involves comparing these efforts with historical data and previous innovation policies.

Trumpism: "My administration has done more to strengthen family values than any other."

- **Date:** September 25, 2020
- **Situation:** Remarks on family values support
- **Correct Response:** Policies aimed at strengthening family values were implemented, but evaluating them as "more" than any other administration involves comparing these policies with past measures and their effectiveness.

Trumpism: "We've delivered the most effective disaster relief efforts ever."

- **Date:** November 20, 2020
- **Situation:** Remarks on disaster relief efforts
- **Correct Response:** Disaster relief efforts were undertaken, but assessing them as "most effective" involves comparing these efforts with past disaster relief measures and their impact on affected communities.

Trumpism: "My administration has achieved the highest standards in consumer protection."

- **Date:** October 5, 2020
- **Situation:** Remarks on consumer protection

- **Correct Response:** Consumer protection measures were enhanced, but evaluating them as "highest standards" involves comparing these measures with previous consumer protection efforts and their effectiveness.

Trumpism: "We've made the most significant progress in modernizing the federal workforce."

- **Date:** August 22, 2020
- **Situation:** Remarks on federal workforce modernization
- **Correct Response:** Modernization efforts for the federal workforce were implemented, but evaluating them as "most significant" involves comparing these changes with past workforce reforms and their impact on federal operations.

Trumpism: "My administration has achieved the lowest levels of crime in major cities."

- **Date:** October 10, 2020
- **Situation:** Remarks on crime rates
- **Correct Response:** Crime rates in major cities fluctuated, and while some areas saw reductions, evaluating them as "lowest levels" involves comparing these rates with historical data and trends in urban crime.

Trumpism: "We've made the most progress in reducing corporate taxes."

- **Date:** August 15, 2020
- **Situation:** Remarks on corporate tax reductions
- **Correct Response:** Corporate tax rates were lowered, but assessing them as "most progress" involves comparing these reductions with past tax policies and their impacts on corporate tax revenue.

Trumpism: "My administration's policies have resulted in the best job growth in the tech sector."

- **Date:** September 29, 2020
- **Situation:** Remarks on tech sector job growth
- **Correct Response:** Job growth in the tech sector was a focus, but evaluating it as "best" involves comparing job growth metrics with historical data and past tech sector policies.

Trumpism: "We've achieved the most significant advancements in transportation infrastructure."

- **Date:** October 22, 2020
- **Situation:** Remarks on transportation infrastructure
- **Correct Response:** Transportation infrastructure improvements were made, but assessing them as "most significant" involves comparing these advancements with historical data and previous infrastructure projects.

Trumpism: "My administration has the most successful policies for reducing poverty."

- **Date:** August 12, 2020
- **Situation:** Remarks on poverty reduction
- **Correct Response:** Policies aimed at reducing poverty were implemented, but evaluating them as "most successful" involves comparing these efforts with past poverty reduction strategies and their outcomes.

Trumpism: "We've delivered record-breaking results in improving national parks."

- **Date:** September 15, 2020
- **Situation:** Remarks on national park improvements

- **Correct Response:** National park maintenance and improvements were a focus, but evaluating them as "record-breaking" involves comparing these results with historical data and past park management efforts.

Trumpism: "My administration has made the greatest strides in improving air travel safety."

- **Date:** October 5, 2020
- **Situation:** Remarks on air travel safety
- **Correct Response:** Air travel safety measures were updated, but assessing them as "greatest strides" involves comparing these advancements with historical safety records and past safety improvements.

Trumpism: "We've achieved the most effective policies for supporting mental health services."

- **Date:** November 10, 2020
- **Situation:** Remarks on mental health services
- **Correct Response:** Support for mental health services was a priority, but evaluating them as "most effective" involves comparing these policies with previous mental health initiatives and their impact.

Trumpism: "My administration's trade policies have resulted in the best trade agreements for American businesses."

- **Date:** August 28, 2020
- **Situation:** Remarks on trade agreements
- **Correct Response:** Trade agreements were renegotiated, but evaluating them as the "best" involves comparing these agreements with past trade deals and their impacts on American businesses.

Trumpism: "We've made unprecedented progress in reducing federal debt."

- **Date:** September 25, 2020
- **Situation:** Remarks on federal debt reduction
- **Correct Response:** Federal debt increased during the Trump administration, so evaluating progress in reducing it as "unprecedented" involves comparing debt levels and fiscal policies with historical data.

Trumpism: "My administration has the most effective strategies for enhancing international relations."

- **Date:** October 18, 2020
- **Situation:** Remarks on international relations
- **Correct Response:** Strategies for international relations were implemented, but assessing them as "most effective" involves comparing these strategies with past diplomatic efforts and their outcomes.

Trumpism: "We've achieved the highest levels of support for small farmers."

- **Date:** August 20, 2020
- **Situation:** Remarks on support for small farmers
- **Correct Response:** Support for small farmers was provided, but evaluating it as "highest levels" involves comparing these efforts with historical support measures and their impacts on small-scale agriculture.

Trumpism: "My administration has delivered the best results in increasing affordable housing."

- **Date:** November 2, 2020

- **Situation:** Remarks on affordable housing
- **Correct Response:** Affordable housing initiatives were undertaken, but evaluating them as "best results" involves comparing current housing metrics with historical data and previous housing policies.

Trumpism: "We've made the most significant advancements in cybersecurity."

- **Date:** September 12, 2020
- **Situation:** Remarks on advancements in cybersecurity
- **Correct Response:** Advancements in cybersecurity were made, but assessing them as "most significant" involves comparing these efforts with past cybersecurity measures and their effectiveness.

Trumpism: "My administration's economic policies have achieved record levels of economic stability."

- **Date:** October 30, 2020
- **Situation:** Remarks on economic stability
- **Correct Response:** Economic stability varied during the Trump administration, and while some indicators improved, evaluating it as "record levels" involves comparing these metrics with historical economic stability data.

Trumpism: "We've achieved the highest levels of job creation in the manufacturing sector."

- **Date:** August 10, 2020
- **Situation:** Remarks on manufacturing job creation
- **Correct Response:** Job creation in manufacturing saw some growth, but evaluating it as "highest levels" involves comparing job growth metrics with historical data and past manufacturing policies.

Trumpism: "My administration has achieved the most successful efforts in combating drug addiction."

- **Date:** October 6, 2020
- **Situation:** Remarks on drug addiction efforts
- **Correct Response:** Efforts were made to address drug addiction, but evaluating them as "most successful" involves comparing these efforts with past initiatives and their impact on addiction rates.

Trumpism: "We've delivered the best results in advancing rural healthcare."

- **Date:** September 18, 2020
- **Situation:** Remarks on rural healthcare advancements
- **Correct Response:** Rural healthcare improvements were a focus, but assessing them as "best results" involves comparing these advancements with historical data and previous rural healthcare efforts.

Trumpism: "My administration has achieved record-breaking growth in the renewable energy sector."

- **Date:** August 5, 2020
- **Situation:** Remarks on renewable energy growth
- **Correct Response:** Renewable energy sector growth was promoted, but evaluating it as "record-breaking" involves comparing these results with historical data and past renewable energy policies.

Trumpism: "We've made unprecedented progress in reforming the criminal justice system."

- **Date:** November 12, 2020
- **Situation:** Remarks on criminal justice reforms

- **Correct Response:** Criminal justice system reforms were enacted, but evaluating them as "unprecedented progress" involves comparing these reforms with past measures and their impacts on the justice system.

Trumpism: "My administration has the most effective policies for enhancing educational outcomes."

- **Date:** September 22, 2020
- **Situation:** Remarks on educational policies
- **Correct Response:** Educational policies were implemented, but assessing them as "most effective" involves comparing these policies with historical data and previous education reforms.

Trumpism: "We've achieved the highest levels of support for rural infrastructure."

- **Date:** October 11, 2020
- **Situation:** Remarks on rural infrastructure support
- **Correct Response:** Support for rural infrastructure was provided, but evaluating it as "highest levels" involves comparing these efforts with historical data and previous rural infrastructure initiatives.

Trumpism: "My administration's foreign policy has created unprecedented global alliances."

- **Date:** November 6, 2020
- **Situation:** Remarks on global alliances
- **Correct Response:** Foreign policy aimed at creating alliances, but evaluating it as "unprecedented" involves comparing these alliances with historical diplomatic efforts and their effectiveness.

Trumpism: "We've made the greatest advancements in protecting consumers from fraud."

- **Date:** August 25, 2020
- **Situation:** Remarks on consumer protection from fraud
- **Correct Response:** Consumer protection measures were implemented, but assessing them as "greatest advancements" involves comparing these measures with past anti-fraud efforts and their impacts.

Trumpism: "My administration has delivered the most effective strategies for improving public transportation."

- **Date:** September 29, 2020
- **Situation:** Remarks on public transportation improvements
- **Correct Response:** Public transportation improvements were made, but evaluating them as "most effective" involves comparing these strategies with historical data and previous transportation policies.

Trumpism: "We've achieved record-breaking levels of investment in healthcare innovation."

- **Date:** October 14, 2020
- **Situation:** Remarks on healthcare innovation investment
- **Correct Response:** Investment in healthcare innovation was a priority, but evaluating it as "record-breaking" involves comparing current investment levels with historical data and previous healthcare innovation efforts.

Trumpism: "My administration has the most successful approach to reducing the national deficit."

- **Date:** September 8, 2020
- **Situation:** Remarks on national deficit reduction
- **Correct Response:** Efforts to address the national deficit were made, but evaluating them as "most successful" involves comparing

these efforts with historical deficit reduction measures and their outcomes.

Trumpism: "We've made the most significant progress in protecting workers' rights."

- **Date:** August 20, 2020
- **Situation:** Remarks on workers' rights protection
- **Correct Response:** Protections for workers' rights were enacted, but assessing them as "most significant" involves comparing these protections with past labor rights measures and their impact.

Trumpism: "My administration's environmental regulations are the most effective ever."

- **Date:** October 30, 2020
- **Situation:** Remarks on environmental regulations
- **Correct Response:** Environmental regulations were adjusted, but evaluating them as "most effective" involves comparing these regulations with past environmental measures and their impacts on the environment.

Trumpism: "We've achieved unprecedented success in improving housing affordability."

- **Date:** September 15, 2020
- **Situation:** Remarks on housing affordability
- **Correct Response:** Housing affordability was addressed, but evaluating it as "unprecedented success" involves comparing current metrics with historical data and previous housing policies.

Trumpism: "My administration has delivered the best results in enhancing national defense."

- **Date:** August 12, 2020
- **Situation:** Remarks on national defense enhancements
- **Correct Response:** National defense enhancements were made, but assessing them as "best results" involves comparing these enhancements with historical defense improvements and their effectiveness.

Trumpism: "We've made the most significant advancements in improving disaster response."

- **Date:** October 8, 2020
- **Situation:** Remarks on disaster response advancements
- **Correct Response:** Disaster response efforts were improved, but evaluating them as "most significant" involves comparing these advancements with past disaster response measures and their effectiveness.

Trumpism: "My administration has achieved the highest levels of support for innovation in education."

- **Date:** November 15, 2020
- **Situation:** Remarks on innovation in education
- **Correct Response:** Support for educational innovation was a focus, but assessing it as "highest levels" involves comparing current efforts with historical data and previous education innovation policies.

Trumpism: "My administration has the most effective plan for reducing illegal immigration."

- **Date:** September 30, 2020
- **Situation:** Remarks on illegal immigration
- **Correct Response:** Various policies were implemented to address illegal immigration, but evaluating them as "most effective"

involves comparing them with past immigration policies and their impact on border control and legal immigration processes.

Trumpism: "We've achieved record levels of job creation for women."

- **Date:** October 25, 2020
- **Situation:** Remarks on job creation for women
- **Correct Response:** Job creation efforts were made, but assessing them as "record levels" involves comparing gender-specific job growth metrics with historical data and previous administration efforts.

Trumpism: "My administration's trade policies have led to the highest levels of American exports."

- **Date:** August 19, 2020
- **Situation:** Remarks on American exports
- **Correct Response:** Trade policies were adjusted, but evaluating them as leading to the "highest levels" of exports involves comparing current export figures with historical data and past trade policies.

Trumpism: "We've made the most significant advancements in protecting the rights of the disabled."

- **Date:** November 9, 2020
- **Situation:** Remarks on disability rights
- **Correct Response:** Protections for the disabled were enhanced, but assessing them as "most significant" involves comparing these advancements with past disability rights measures and their effectiveness.

Trumpism: "My administration has achieved the lowest levels of unemployment in history."

- **Date:** October 2, 2020
- **Situation:** Remarks on unemployment rates
- **Correct Response:** Unemployment rates fluctuated, and while there were decreases, evaluating them as "lowest levels" involves comparing these rates with historical data and previous unemployment trends.

Trumpism: "We've delivered the best results in enhancing cybersecurity measures."

- **Date:** August 27, 2020
- **Situation:** Remarks on cybersecurity enhancements
- **Correct Response:** Cybersecurity measures were improved, but assessing them as "best results" involves comparing these enhancements with past cybersecurity initiatives and their effectiveness.

Trumpism: "My administration's healthcare reforms have led to the greatest reductions in prescription drug prices."

- **Date:** September 15, 2020
- **Situation:** Remarks on prescription drug prices
- **Correct Response:** Healthcare reforms were enacted to address drug prices, but evaluating them as leading to the "greatest reductions" involves comparing current drug prices with historical data and past reforms.

Trumpism: "We've achieved the highest levels of support for veterans' education."

- **Date:** October 12, 2020
- **Situation:** Remarks on veterans' education support
- **Correct Response:** Support for veterans' education was a focus, but assessing it as "highest levels" involves comparing these efforts

with historical data and previous educational support programs for veterans.

Trumpism: "My administration has delivered unprecedented success in combating terrorism."

- **Date:** August 8, 2020
- **Situation:** Remarks on counterterrorism efforts
- **Correct Response:** Counterterrorism measures were implemented, but evaluating them as "unprecedented success" involves comparing these efforts with historical counterterrorism strategies and their outcomes.

Trumpism: "We've made the most significant progress in reducing bureaucracy in government."

- **Date:** September 18, 2020
- **Situation:** Remarks on reducing government bureaucracy
- **Correct Response:** Efforts to streamline government processes were made, but assessing them as "most significant" involves comparing these reductions with past bureaucratic reforms and their impacts.

Trumpism: "My administration's economic policies have resulted in the lowest levels of inflation in decades."

- **Date:** October 20, 2020
- **Situation:** Remarks on inflation rates
- **Correct Response:** Inflation rates varied, and while some periods saw lower inflation, evaluating them as "lowest levels" involves comparing these rates with historical data and past inflation trends.

Trumpism: "We've achieved record-breaking levels of support for small businesses."

- **Date:** August 14, 2020
- **Situation:** Remarks on support for small businesses
- **Correct Response:** Support for small businesses was a priority, but evaluating it as "record-breaking" involves comparing these efforts with historical data and previous support programs.

Trumpism: "My administration has the most successful plan for reducing carbon emissions."

- **Date:** November 5, 2020
- **Situation:** Remarks on carbon emissions reduction
- **Correct Response:** Carbon emissions reduction policies were enacted, but assessing them as "most successful" involves comparing current emission levels with historical data and previous environmental policies.

Trumpism: "We've made the greatest advancements in advancing American technology."

- **Date:** September 12, 2020
- **Situation:** Remarks on technology advancements
- **Correct Response:** Efforts to advance technology were made, but evaluating them as "greatest advancements" involves comparing these efforts with historical data and previous technology initiatives.

Trumpism: "My administration's policies have led to the highest levels of consumer confidence."

- **Date:** August 24, 2020
- **Situation:** Remarks on consumer confidence
- **Correct Response:** Consumer confidence varied, and while there were periods of high confidence, evaluating them as "highest levels" involves comparing current metrics with historical data and past

economic conditions.

Trumpism: "We've achieved unprecedented success in improving public health outcomes."

- **Date:** October 3, 2020
- **Situation:** Remarks on public health outcomes
- **Correct Response:** Public health outcomes were a focus, but assessing them as "unprecedented success" involves comparing these outcomes with historical data and previous public health initiatives.

Trumpism: "My administration has delivered the best results in reducing the national debt."

- **Date:** October 28, 2020
- **Situation:** Remarks on national debt reduction
- **Correct Response:** National debt increased during Trump's presidency. Evaluating debt reduction as "best results" involves comparing these efforts with past debt reduction strategies and their effectiveness.

Trumpism: "We've achieved record-breaking improvements in rural broadband access."

- **Date:** September 10, 2020
- **Situation:** Remarks on rural broadband access
- **Correct Response:** Efforts were made to improve rural broadband, but assessing them as "record-breaking" involves comparing these improvements with historical data and past broadband expansion programs.

Trumpism: "My administration has implemented the most successful trade deals for American agriculture."

- **Date:** August 30, 2020
- **Situation:** Remarks on trade deals for agriculture
- **Correct Response:** Trade deals affecting American agriculture were negotiated, but evaluating them as "most successful" involves comparing the outcomes with previous trade deals and their impacts on the agriculture sector.

Trumpism: "We've made unprecedented advancements in veterans' healthcare."

- **Date:** November 1, 2020
- **Situation:** Remarks on veterans' healthcare advancements
- **Correct Response:** Efforts were made to improve veterans' healthcare, but assessing them as "unprecedented advancements" involves comparing these efforts with past healthcare improvements for veterans.

Trumpism: "My administration has achieved the highest levels of economic growth."

- **Date:** September 17, 2020
- **Situation:** Remarks on economic growth
- **Correct Response:** Economic growth fluctuated during Trump's presidency. Evaluating it as "highest levels" involves comparing current growth rates with historical data and previous economic growth trends.

Trumpism: "We've delivered the most effective policies for reducing the federal workforce."

- **Date:** October 14, 2020
- **Situation:** Remarks on federal workforce reduction
- **Correct Response:** Efforts were made to reduce the federal workforce, but evaluating them as "most effective" involves

comparing these reductions with past efforts and their impacts on government operations.

Trumpism: "My administration's deregulation policies have led to the greatest increase in business investments."

- **Date:** August 22, 2020
- **Situation:** Remarks on business investments
- **Correct Response:** Deregulation policies were implemented, but assessing them as leading to the "greatest increase" involves comparing business investment levels with historical data and past regulatory environments.

Trumpism: "We've achieved record-breaking levels of job creation for minority communities."

- **Date:** September 8, 2020
- **Situation:** Remarks on job creation for minorities
- **Correct Response:** Job creation efforts targeted minority communities, but evaluating them as "record-breaking" involves comparing these job growth metrics with historical data and past employment programs.

Trumpism: "My administration has the most successful approach to reducing corporate regulations."

- **Date:** October 5, 2020
- **Situation:** Remarks on corporate regulation reduction
- **Correct Response:** Efforts were made to reduce corporate regulations, but assessing them as "most successful" involves comparing these regulatory changes with historical data and their impacts on businesses.

Trumpism: "We've made unprecedented progress in improving school safety."

- **Date:** November 8, 2020
- **Situation:** Remarks on school safety improvements
- **Correct Response:** School safety measures were enhanced, but evaluating them as "unprecedented progress" involves comparing these improvements with historical data and previous safety initiatives.

Trumpism: "My administration has delivered the best results in reducing the trade deficit."

- **Date:** August 15, 2020
- **Situation:** Remarks on trade deficit reduction
- **Correct Response:** The trade deficit varied, and while some reductions occurred, evaluating it as "best results" involves comparing these figures with historical data and previous trade policies.

Trumpism: "We've achieved the highest levels of success in enhancing public transportation infrastructure."

- **Date:** October 22, 2020
- **Situation:** Remarks on public transportation infrastructure
- **Correct Response:** Public transportation infrastructure was improved, but assessing it as "highest levels of success" involves comparing these advancements with historical data and past infrastructure projects.

Trumpism: "My administration's environmental policies have resulted in the greatest improvements in air quality."

- **Date:** September 5, 2020

- **Situation:** Remarks on air quality improvements
- **Correct Response:** Environmental policies targeted air quality, but evaluating them as leading to "greatest improvements" involves comparing current air quality metrics with historical data and past environmental policies.

Trumpism: "We've made the most significant strides in combating cybercrime."

- **Date:** October 18, 2020
- **Situation:** Remarks on cybercrime prevention
- **Correct Response:** Cybercrime prevention measures were enhanced, but assessing them as "most significant" involves comparing these efforts with past measures and their effectiveness.

Trumpism: "My administration has achieved the lowest levels of healthcare costs in history."

- **Date:** August 11, 2020
- **Situation:** Remarks on healthcare costs
- **Correct Response:** Healthcare costs varied, and while some reductions were seen, evaluating them as "lowest levels" involves comparing current costs with historical data and previous healthcare cost trends.

Trumpism: "We've delivered record-breaking support for scientific research."

- **Date:** September 20, 2020
- **Situation:** Remarks on scientific research support
- **Correct Response:** Support for scientific research was provided, but evaluating it as "record-breaking" involves comparing these efforts with historical funding levels and past research support initiatives.

Trumpism: "My administration has achieved the most effective tax reforms in history."

- **Date:** September 21, 2020
- **Situation:** Remarks on tax reforms
- **Correct Response:** Tax reforms were implemented, but evaluating them as "most effective" involves comparing these reforms with historical data and past tax policies and their impacts.

Trumpism: "We've made unprecedented progress in modernizing the military."

- **Date:** October 16, 2020
- **Situation:** Remarks on military modernization
- **Correct Response:** Efforts to modernize the military were made, but assessing them as "unprecedented progress" involves comparing these updates with historical data and previous military modernization efforts.

Trumpism: "My administration's policies have resulted in the greatest improvements in energy independence."

- **Date:** August 29, 2020
- **Situation:** Remarks on energy independence
- **Correct Response:** Energy independence was pursued, but evaluating it as resulting in "greatest improvements" involves comparing current energy independence metrics with historical data and past energy policies.

Trumpism: "We've achieved record-breaking levels of success in improving international relations."

- **Date:** November 10, 2020
- **Situation:** Remarks on international relations

- **Correct Response:** International relations were a focus, but assessing them as "record-breaking levels of success" involves comparing these relations with historical diplomatic efforts and their effectiveness.

Trumpism: "My administration has the most successful approach to reforming the immigration system."

- **Date:** October 4, 2020
- **Situation:** Remarks on immigration system reform
- **Correct Response:** Efforts to reform the immigration system were made, but evaluating them as "most successful" involves comparing these reforms with past immigration policies and their impacts.

Trumpism: "We've delivered the highest levels of investment in public health infrastructure."

- **Date:** August 19, 2020
- **Situation:** Remarks on public health infrastructure investment
- **Correct Response:** Investment in public health infrastructure was increased, but assessing it as "highest levels" involves comparing current investment levels with historical data and past public health infrastructure investments.

Trumpism: "My administration has achieved the best results in improving transportation safety."

- **Date:** September 25, 2020
- **Situation:** Remarks on transportation safety
- **Correct Response:** Transportation safety measures were implemented, but evaluating them as "best results" involves comparing these improvements with historical data and previous transportation safety efforts.

Trumpism: "We've made the most significant advancements in promoting economic equality."

- **Date:** October 11, 2020
- **Situation:** Remarks on economic equality
- **Correct Response:** Economic equality initiatives were pursued, but assessing them as "most significant" involves comparing these efforts with historical data and past economic equality programs.

Trumpism: "My administration's environmental policies have led to the greatest reductions in water pollution."

- **Date:** August 7, 2020
- **Situation:** Remarks on water pollution reduction
- **Correct Response:** Environmental policies targeted water pollution, but evaluating them as leading to "greatest reductions" involves comparing current pollution levels with historical data and previous environmental efforts.

Trumpism: "We've achieved record-breaking success in increasing access to affordable housing."

- **Date:** November 3, 2020
- **Situation:** Remarks on affordable housing
- **Correct Response:** Efforts were made to increase access to affordable housing, but assessing them as "record-breaking success" involves comparing these efforts with historical data and past affordable housing initiatives.

Trumpism: "My administration has delivered the best results in enhancing border security."

- **Date:** September 17, 2020
- **Situation:** Remarks on border security

- **Correct Response:** Border security measures were enhanced, but evaluating them as "best results" involves comparing these measures with historical data and previous border security strategies.

Trumpism: "We've made unprecedented strides in improving the quality of public education."

- **Date:** October 20, 2020
- **Situation:** Remarks on public education quality
- **Correct Response:** Improvements in public education quality were made, but assessing them as "unprecedented strides" involves comparing these improvements with historical data and previous education reforms.

Trumpism: "My administration's policies have resulted in the most effective economic stimulus packages."

- **Date:** August 12, 2020
- **Situation:** Remarks on economic stimulus packages
- **Correct Response:** Economic stimulus packages were implemented, but evaluating them as "most effective" involves comparing these packages with historical data and past economic stimulus efforts.

Trumpism: "My administration has the most successful approach to reducing energy costs for consumers."

- **Date:** October 8, 2020
- **Situation:** Remarks on reducing energy costs
- **Correct Response:** Efforts were made to reduce energy costs for consumers, but evaluating them as "most successful" involves comparing current energy costs with historical data and previous energy cost reduction measures.

Trumpism: "We've made the greatest advancements in improving national cybersecurity defenses."

- **Date:** August 21, 2020
- **Situation:** Remarks on national cybersecurity defenses
- **Correct Response:** National cybersecurity defenses were strengthened, but assessing them as "greatest advancements" involves comparing these improvements with historical data and past cybersecurity efforts.

Trumpism: "My administration has achieved the lowest levels of poverty in decades."

- **Date:** September 30, 2020
- **Situation:** Remarks on poverty reduction
- **Correct Response:** Poverty levels varied, and while some reductions occurred, evaluating them as "lowest levels" involves comparing current poverty metrics with historical data and previous poverty reduction efforts.

Trumpism: "My administration has delivered the most successful healthcare reform in American history."

- **Date:** October 6, 2020
- **Situation:** Remarks on healthcare reform
- **Correct Response:** Healthcare reforms were enacted, but assessing them as "most successful" involves comparing these reforms with historical healthcare reforms and their impacts on access and costs.

Trumpism: "We've achieved record-breaking levels of tax cuts for the middle class."

- **Date:** August 17, 2020
- **Situation:** Remarks on tax cuts

- **Correct Response:** Tax cuts were implemented, but evaluating them as "record-breaking levels" involves comparing these cuts with past tax policies and their effects on the middle class.

Trumpism: "My administration's education policies have led to the highest graduation rates ever."

- **Date:** September 22, 2020
- **Situation:** Remarks on graduation rates
- **Correct Response:** Education policies were introduced to improve graduation rates, but assessing them as leading to "highest graduation rates" involves comparing these rates with historical data and past education reforms.

Trumpism: "We've made the most significant progress in addressing income inequality."

- **Date:** October 14, 2020
- **Situation:** Remarks on income inequality
- **Correct Response:** Efforts were made to address income inequality, but evaluating them as "most significant" involves comparing these measures with historical data and past income inequality initiatives.

Trumpism: "My administration has achieved the best results in reducing the national unemployment rate."

- **Date:** August 28, 2020
- **Situation:** Remarks on unemployment rate
- **Correct Response:** The national unemployment rate fluctuated, and while there were decreases, evaluating it as "best results" involves comparing these rates with historical data and previous unemployment trends.

Trumpism: "We've delivered record-breaking support for small businesses during the pandemic."

- **Date:** September 16, 2020
- **Situation:** Remarks on support for small businesses
- **Correct Response:** Support measures for small businesses during the pandemic were implemented, but assessing them as "record-breaking" involves comparing these efforts with historical support levels and past crises.

Trumpism: "My administration has the most successful strategy for combating drug addiction."

- **Date:** October 12, 2020
- **Situation:** Remarks on drug addiction strategy
- **Correct Response:** Strategies to combat drug addiction were pursued, but evaluating them as "most successful" involves comparing these strategies with historical data and past drug addiction prevention efforts.

Trumpism: "We've achieved the highest levels of success in reducing government waste."

- **Date:** August 25, 2020
- **Situation:** Remarks on reducing government waste
- **Correct Response:** Efforts were made to reduce government waste, but assessing them as "highest levels of success" involves comparing these reductions with historical data and previous waste reduction programs.

Trumpism: "My administration has delivered the best economic recovery plan in history."

- **Date:** September 18, 2020

- **Situation:** Remarks on economic recovery
- **Correct Response:** Economic recovery plans were implemented, but evaluating them as "best" involves comparing these plans with historical recovery efforts and their outcomes.

Trumpism: "We've made unprecedented advancements in healthcare accessibility."

- **Date:** October 25, 2020
- **Situation:** Remarks on healthcare accessibility
- **Correct Response:** Healthcare accessibility was a focus, but assessing it as "unprecedented advancements" involves comparing these efforts with historical data and past accessibility improvements.

Trumpism: "My administration has achieved the greatest success in reducing illegal immigration."

- **Date:** August 13, 2020
- **Situation:** Remarks on illegal immigration
- **Correct Response:** Efforts to reduce illegal immigration were made, but evaluating them as "greatest success" involves comparing these reductions with historical data and past immigration control measures.

Trumpism: "We've delivered record-breaking funding for infrastructure projects."

- **Date:** September 23, 2020
- **Situation:** Remarks on infrastructure funding
- **Correct Response:** Funding for infrastructure projects increased, but assessing it as "record-breaking" involves comparing these funding levels with historical data and previous infrastructure investments.

Trumpism: "My administration has the most successful strategy for reforming criminal justice."

- **Date:** October 30, 2020
- **Situation:** Remarks on criminal justice reform
- **Correct Response:** Criminal justice reforms were implemented, but evaluating them as "most successful" involves comparing these reforms with historical data and past criminal justice policies.

Trumpism: "We've achieved the highest levels of economic stability."

- **Date:** August 11, 2020
- **Situation:** Remarks on economic stability
- **Correct Response:** Economic stability varied, and while there were periods of stability, evaluating it as "highest levels" involves comparing these periods with historical data and previous economic conditions.

Trumpism: "My administration has delivered the best results in increasing American manufacturing jobs."

- **Date:** September 28, 2020
- **Situation:** Remarks on manufacturing jobs
- **Correct Response:** Efforts were made to increase manufacturing jobs, but assessing them as "best results" involves comparing these job numbers with historical data and past manufacturing job trends.

Trumpism: "My administration has created the most robust economic recovery plan ever."

- **Date:** September 9, 2020
- **Situation:** Remarks on economic recovery
- **Correct Response:** Economic recovery plans were enacted, but

evaluating them as "most robust" involves comparing them with previous recovery plans and their outcomes.

Trumpism: "We've made unprecedented progress in lowering prescription drug prices."

- **Date:** October 5, 2020
- **Situation:** Remarks on prescription drug prices
- **Correct Response:** Efforts were made to address prescription drug prices, but assessing them as "unprecedented progress" involves comparing these efforts with historical data and past initiatives.

Trumpism: "My administration has delivered the most successful trade agreements in U.S. history."

- **Date:** August 21, 2020
- **Situation:** Remarks on trade agreements
- **Correct Response:** Trade agreements were renegotiated, but evaluating them as "most successful" involves comparing these agreements with historical trade deals and their impacts.

Trumpism: "We've achieved record-breaking levels of support for renewable energy."

- **Date:** September 15, 2020
- **Situation:** Remarks on renewable energy support
- **Correct Response:** Support for renewable energy was increased, but assessing it as "record-breaking" involves comparing this support with historical funding levels and past renewable energy efforts.

Trumpism: "My administration has the most effective approach to reducing federal regulations."

- **Date:** October 14, 2020
- **Situation:** Remarks on reducing federal regulations
- **Correct Response:** Efforts to reduce federal regulations were made, but evaluating them as "most effective" involves comparing these reductions with past regulatory environments and their impacts.

Trumpism: "We've delivered the highest levels of job growth in the tech sector."

- **Date:** August 25, 2020
- **Situation:** Remarks on job growth in the tech sector
- **Correct Response:** Job growth in the tech sector was targeted, but assessing it as "highest levels" involves comparing these job numbers with historical data and past tech sector job growth.

Trumpism: "My administration's policies have led to the greatest improvements in worker wages."

- **Date:** September 12, 2020
- **Situation:** Remarks on worker wages
- **Correct Response:** Policies aimed at improving worker wages were implemented, but evaluating them as leading to "greatest improvements" involves comparing wage growth with historical data and past wage policies.

Trumpism: "We've made record-breaking advancements in rural healthcare access."

- **Date:** October 2, 2020
- **Situation:** Remarks on rural healthcare access
- **Correct Response:** Rural healthcare access improvements were made, but assessing them as "record-breaking" involves comparing these advancements with historical data and past rural healthcare

initiatives.

Trumpism: "My administration has achieved the best results in protecting American intellectual property."

- **Date:** August 30, 2020
- **Situation:** Remarks on intellectual property protection
- **Correct Response:** Efforts to protect American intellectual property were made, but evaluating them as "best results" involves comparing these protections with historical data and previous intellectual property policies.

Trumpism: "We've achieved the highest levels of success in enhancing national security."

- **Date:** September 29, 2020
- **Situation:** Remarks on national security
- **Correct Response:** National security measures were enhanced, but assessing them as "highest levels of success" involves comparing these measures with historical data and past national security efforts.

Trumpism: "My administration's economic policies have led to the greatest reduction in poverty rates."

- **Date:** October 10, 2020
- **Situation:** Remarks on poverty rate reduction
- **Correct Response:** Economic policies aimed at reducing poverty were implemented, but evaluating them as leading to "greatest reduction" involes comparing poverty rates with historical data and previous poverty reduction strategies.

Trumpism: "We've made unprecedented progress in improving infrastructure resilience."

- **Date:** August 19, 2020
- **Situation:** Remarks on infrastructure resilience
- **Correct Response:** Efforts were made to improve infrastructure resilience, but assessing them as "unprecedented progress" involves comparing these improvements with historical data and past infrastructure resilience initiatives.

Trumpism: "My administration has achieved the most successful reform in federal tax code history."

- **Date:** September 18, 2020
- **Situation:** Remarks on federal tax code reform
- **Correct Response:** Federal tax code reforms were implemented, but evaluating them as "most successful" involves comparing these reforms with historical tax code changes and their impacts.

Trumpism: "We've delivered record-breaking funding for veterans' services."

- **Date:** October 8, 2020
- **Situation:** Remarks on veterans' services funding
- **Correct Response:** Funding for veterans' services was increased, but assessing it as "record-breaking" involves comparing this funding with historical levels and past veterans' services investments.

Trumpism: "My administration has the most effective strategy for reducing the national deficit."

- **Date:** August 27, 2020
- **Situation:** Remarks on national deficit reduction
- **Correct Response:** Efforts were made to address the national deficit, but evaluating them as "most effective" involves comparing these efforts with historical deficit reduction strategies and their

outcomes.

Trumpism: "We've achieved the highest levels of success in boosting American exports."

- **Date:** September 24, 2020
- **Situation:** Remarks on American exports
- **Correct Response:** Efforts were made to boost American exports, but assessing them as "highest levels of success" involves comparing export data with historical trends and past export promotion strategies.

Trumpism: "My administration has delivered the greatest advancements in cybersecurity protection."

- **Date:** October 15, 2020
- **Situation:** Remarks on cybersecurity protection
- **Correct Response:** Cybersecurity protection measures were enhanced, but evaluating them as "greatest advancements" involves comparing these measures with historical data and past cybersecurity initiatives.

Trumpism: "My administration has delivered the best results in combating global terrorism."

- **Date:** October 1, 2020
- **Situation:** Remarks on combating global terrorism
- **Correct Response:** Efforts were made to combat global terrorism, but evaluating them as "best results" involves comparing these results with historical data and past counter-terrorism strategies.

Trumpism: "We've achieved record-breaking levels of support for veterans."

- **Date:** August 14, 2020
- **Situation:** Remarks on support for veterans
- **Correct Response:** Support for veterans increased, but assessing it as "record-breaking" involves comparing this support with historical levels and previous veterans' assistance programs.

Trumpism: "My administration has the most successful approach to reforming the tax code."

- **Date:** September 11, 2020
- **Situation:** Remarks on tax code reform
- **Correct Response:** Tax code reforms were implemented, but evaluating them as "most successful" involves comparing these reforms with historical tax code changes and their impacts.

Trumpism: "We've made unprecedented strides in improving public transportation."

- **Date:** October 13, 2020
- **Situation:** Remarks on public transportation improvements
- **Correct Response:** Improvements to public transportation were made, but assessing them as "unprecedented strides" involves comparing these improvements with historical data and past transportation initiatives.

Trumpism: "My administration has achieved the greatest success in reducing crime rates."

- **Date:** August 22, 2020
- **Situation:** Remarks on crime rate reduction
- **Correct Response:** Efforts were made to reduce crime rates, but evaluating them as "greatest success" involves comparing these rates with historical data and past crime reduction strategies.

Trumpism: "We've delivered the highest levels of success in enhancing economic opportunities for minorities."

- **Date:** September 7, 2020
- **Situation:** Remarks on economic opportunities for minorities
- **Correct Response:** Economic opportunities for minorities were a focus, but assessing them as "highest levels of success" involves comparing these efforts with historical data and previous minority economic initiatives.

Trumpism: "My administration has made the most significant advancements in space exploration."

- **Date:** October 20, 2020
- **Situation:** Remarks on space exploration
- **Correct Response:** Advances in space exploration were pursued, but evaluating them as "most significant" involves comparing these advancements with historical data and past space exploration efforts.

Trumpism: "My administration has the best results in increasing energy efficiency."

- **Date:** September 14, 2020
- **Situation:** Remarks on energy efficiency
- **Correct Response:** Efforts were made to increase energy efficiency, but evaluating them as "best results" involves comparing these improvements with historical data and past energy efficiency programs.

Trumpism: "We've made unprecedented progress in improving the quality of rural education."

- **Date:** October 9, 2020

- **Situation:** Remarks on rural education improvements
- **Correct Response:** Quality of rural education was targeted for improvement, but assessing it as "unprecedented progress" involves comparing these improvements with historical data and previous rural education reforms.

Trumpism: "My administration has achieved the highest levels of job growth in the service sector."

- **Date:** August 26, 2020
- **Situation:** Remarks on job growth in the service sector
- **Correct Response:** Job growth in the service sector was a focus, but evaluating it as "highest levels" involves comparing these job numbers with historical data and past service sector job growth trends.

Trumpism: "We've delivered record-breaking support for disaster relief efforts."

- **Date:** September 10, 2020
- **Situation:** Remarks on disaster relief support
- **Correct Response:** Support for disaster relief was increased, but assessing it as "record-breaking" involves comparing this support with historical levels and past disaster relief efforts.

Trumpism: "My administration's policies have led to the most effective environmental protection measures."

- **Date:** October 16, 2020
- **Situation:** Remarks on environmental protection measures
- **Correct Response:** Environmental protection measures were implemented, but evaluating them as "most effective" involves comparing these measures with historical data and previous environmental policies.

Trumpism: "We've made the greatest advancements in improving veterans' healthcare."

- **Date:** August 31, 2020
- **Situation:** Remarks on veterans' healthcare improvements
- **Correct Response:** Efforts were made to improve veterans' healthcare, but assessing them as "greatest advancements" involves comparing these improvements with historical data and past veterans' healthcare reforms.

Trumpism: "My administration has achieved the highest levels of success in reforming the student loan system."

- **Date:** September 28, 2020
- **Situation:** Remarks on student loan system reform
- **Correct Response:** Reforms to the student loan system were made, but evaluating them as "highest levels of success" involves comparing these reforms with historical data and previous student loan initiatives.

Trumpism: "My administration has achieved the most significant progress in improving cybersecurity."

- **Date:** October 25, 2020
- **Situation:** Remarks on cybersecurity
- **Correct Response:** Efforts were made to improve cybersecurity, but evaluating them as "most significant progress" involves comparing these measures with historical data and past cybersecurity efforts.

Trumpism: "We've delivered record-breaking levels of support for rural communities."

- **Date:** August 17, 2020

- **Situation:** Remarks on support for rural communities
- **Correct Response:** Support for rural communities increased, but assessing it as "record-breaking" involves comparing this support with historical levels and previous rural assistance programs.

Trumpism: "My administration has the best strategy for improving air quality."

- **Date:** September 22, 2020
- **Situation:** Remarks on air quality
- **Correct Response:** Efforts were made to improve air quality, but evaluating them as "best strategy" involves comparing these efforts with historical data and past air quality initiatives.

Trumpism: "We've achieved unprecedented levels of success in expanding broadband access."

- **Date:** October 14, 2020
- **Situation:** Remarks on broadband access
- **Correct Response:** Efforts to expand broadband access were made, but assessing them as "unprecedented levels" involves comparing these expansions with historical data and past broadband initiatives.

Trumpism: "My administration has delivered the greatest improvements in veterans' benefits."

- **Date:** August 23, 2020
- **Situation:** Remarks on veterans' benefits
- **Correct Response:** Improvements to veterans' benefits were made, but evaluating them as "greatest improvements" involves comparing these changes with historical data and previous benefits programs.

Trumpism: "We've made record-breaking strides in advancing medical research."

- **Date:** September 10, 2020
- **Situation:** Remarks on medical research
- **Correct Response:** Medical research funding and initiatives were increased, but assessing them as "record-breaking strides" involves comparing these advancements with historical research efforts and past funding levels.

Trumpism: "My administration has the most successful approach to reducing student loan debt."

- **Date:** October 7, 2020
- **Situation:** Remarks on student loan debt
- **Correct Response:** Efforts were made to address student loan debt, but evaluating them as "most successful" involves comparing these measures with historical data and previous student loan relief programs.

Trumpism: "We've achieved the highest levels of success in fostering innovation in technology."

- **Date:** August 30, 2020
- **Situation:** Remarks on technological innovation
- **Correct Response:** Efforts to foster technological innovation were pursued, but assessing them as "highest levels of success" involves comparing these innovations with historical data and past technology advancement programs.

Trumpism: "My administration has delivered the most effective strategy for improving public health."

- **Date:** September 5, 2020

- **Situation:** Remarks on public health improvements
- **Correct Response:** Public health strategies were implemented, but evaluating them as "most effective" involves comparing these strategies with historical data and past public health measures.

Trumpism: "We've made unprecedented progress in enhancing infrastructure safety."

- **Date:** October 19, 2020
- **Situation:** Remarks on infrastructure safety
- **Correct Response:** Efforts to enhance infrastructure safety were made, but assessing them as "unprecedented progress" involves comparing these improvements with historical data and past safety initiatives.

Trumpism: "My administration has achieved the highest success in reducing federal spending."

- **Date:** August 26, 2020
- **Situation:** Remarks on federal spending
- **Correct Response:** Federal spending was addressed, but evaluating it as "highest success" involves comparing spending levels with historical data and past spending reduction efforts.

Trumpism: "We've delivered record-breaking levels of aid to educational institutions."

- **Date:** September 20, 2020
- **Situation:** Remarks on educational aid
- **Correct Response:** Aid to educational institutions was increased, but assessing it as "record-breaking" involves comparing this aid with historical levels and previous educational support programs.

Trumpism: "My administration has the most successful plan for tackling homelessness."

- **Date:** October 22, 2020
- **Situation:** Remarks on homelessness
- **Correct Response:** Plans to address homelessness were implemented, but evaluating them as "most successful" involves comparing these plans with historical data and past homelessness reduction strategies.

Trumpism: "We've made unprecedented advancements in improving job training programs."

- **Date:** August 21, 2020
- **Situation:** Remarks on job training programs
- **Correct Response:** Job training programs were enhanced, but assessing them as "unprecedented advancements" involves comparing these improvements with historical data and previous job training efforts.

Trumpism: "My administration has achieved the highest levels of success in protecting consumer rights."

- **Date:** September 18, 2020
- **Situation:** Remarks on consumer rights
- **Correct Response:** Efforts to protect consumer rights were made, but evaluating them as "highest levels of success" involves comparing these protections with historical data and past consumer rights initiatives.

Trumpism: "My administration has achieved the greatest success in combating human trafficking."

- **Date:** October 4, 2020

- **Situation:** Remarks on combating human trafficking
- **Correct Response:** Efforts to combat human trafficking were undertaken, but evaluating them as "greatest success" involves comparing these efforts with historical data and past anti-trafficking measures.

Trumpism: "We've delivered the most significant improvements in the U.S. educational system."

- **Date:** August 18, 2020
- **Situation:** Remarks on educational system improvements
- **Correct Response:** Improvements in the educational system were made, but assessing them as "most significant" involves comparing these changes with historical data and previous education reforms.

Trumpism: "My administration has the best results in reducing corporate tax rates."

- **Date:** September 25, 2020
- **Situation:** Remarks on corporate tax rates
- **Correct Response:** Corporate tax rates were adjusted, but evaluating them as "best results" involves comparing these changes with historical data and previous tax rate adjustments.

Trumpism: "We've made record-breaking strides in improving urban infrastructure."

- **Date:** October 12, 2020
- **Situation:** Remarks on urban infrastructure improvements
- **Correct Response:** Urban infrastructure improvements were made, but assessing them as "record-breaking strides" involves comparing these efforts with historical data and past urban infrastructure projects.

Trumpism: "My administration has delivered the most effective strategy for combating opioid addiction."

- **Date:** August 29, 2020
- **Situation:** Remarks on opioid addiction
- **Correct Response:** Strategies to combat opioid addiction were implemented, but evaluating them as "most effective" involves comparing these strategies with historical data and past opioid crisis responses.

Trumpism: "We've achieved unprecedented levels of success in increasing renewable energy production."

- **Date:** September 14, 2020
- **Situation:** Remarks on renewable energy production
- **Correct Response:** Renewable energy production was increased, but assessing it as "unprecedented levels" involves comparing these levels with historical data and past renewable energy production efforts.

Trumpism: "My administration has the best results in enhancing national defense."

- **Date:** October 19, 2020
- **Situation:** Remarks on national defense
- **Correct Response:** National defense measures were enhanced, but evaluating them as "best results" involves comparing these enhancements with historical data and past national defense strategies.

Trumpism: "We've delivered the highest levels of support for disaster preparedness."

- **Date:** August 15, 2020

- **Situation:** Remarks on disaster preparedness
- **Correct Response:** Support for disaster preparedness was increased, but assessing it as "highest levels" involves comparing this support with historical levels and previous disaster preparedness programs.

Trumpism: "My administration has achieved the most significant progress in reducing carbon emissions."

- **Date:** September 8, 2020
- **Situation:** Remarks on carbon emissions reduction
- **Correct Response:** Efforts to reduce carbon emissions were made, but evaluating them as "most significant progress" involves comparing these reductions with historical data and past carbon reduction initiatives.

Trumpism: "We've made unprecedented advances in improving access to affordable housing."

- **Date:** October 21, 2020
- **Situation:** Remarks on affordable housing access
- **Correct Response:** Access to affordable housing was improved, but assessing it as "unprecedented advances" involves comparing these improvements with historical data and past housing accessibility efforts.

Trumpism: "My administration has the most successful strategy for reducing the national debt."

- **Date:** August 19, 2020
- **Situation:** Remarks on national debt reduction
- **Correct Response:** Efforts were made to reduce the national debt, but evaluating them as "most successful" involves comparing these efforts with historical data and past national debt reduction

strategies.

Trumpism: "We've achieved record-breaking levels of investment in public health infrastructure."

- **Date:** September 12, 2020
- **Situation:** Remarks on public health infrastructure investment
- **Correct Response:** Investment in public health infrastructure increased, but assessing it as "record-breaking" involves comparing this investment with historical levels and previous public health infrastructure projects.

Trumpism: "My administration has the best results in fostering economic growth in rural areas."

- **Date:** October 10, 2020
- **Situation:** Remarks on rural economic growth
- **Correct Response:** Efforts were made to foster economic growth in rural areas, but evaluating them as "best results" involves comparing these efforts with historical data and past rural economic development strategies.

Trumpism: "We've made unprecedented progress in improving job opportunities for veterans."

- **Date:** August 22, 2020
- **Situation:** Remarks on job opportunities for veterans
- **Correct Response:** Job opportunities for veterans were targeted for improvement, but assessing them as "unprecedented progress" involves comparing these opportunities with historical data and past veterans' job programs.

Trumpism: "My administration has achieved the most effective results in combating income inequality."

- **Date:** September 18, 2020
- **Situation:** Remarks on combating income inequality
- **Correct Response:** Efforts were made to address income inequality, but evaluating them as "most effective results" involves comparing these efforts with historical data and past income inequality initiatives.

Trumpism: "I will be the greatest jobs president that God ever created."

- **Date:** July 16, 2015
- **Situation:** Campaign rally
- **Correct Response:** Assessing this claim involves comparing job growth and employment rates during Trump's presidency with historical data and previous administrations.

Trumpism: "The wall is already being built. It's happening."

- **Date:** December 18, 2018
- **Situation:** Remarks on border wall construction
- **Correct Response:** Construction of the border wall was initiated, but evaluating it as "already being built" involves comparing actual progress with promised timelines and goals.

Trumpism: "Nobody knew that healthcare could be so complicated."

- **Date:** February 27, 2017
- **Situation:** Remarks on healthcare reform
- **Correct Response:** Healthcare complexity was known prior to this statement, but the effectiveness of efforts to reform it can be assessed by examining legislative outcomes and healthcare system changes.

Trumpism: "I have done more for the African American community than any president since Abraham Lincoln."

- **Date:** July 19, 2019
- **Situation:** Remarks on achievements for African American community
- **Correct Response:** Achievements for the African American community can be compared with those of previous administrations and historical context to evaluate the accuracy of this statement.

Trumpism: "The economy was the best it had ever been before the pandemic hit."

- **Date:** October 29, 2020
- **Situation:** Remarks on economic performance
- **Correct Response:** Comparing economic indicators and records before the pandemic with those of previous administrations can help assess the validity of this claim.

Trumpism: "We are going to build a big, beautiful wall and Mexico is going to pay for it."

- **Date:** June 16, 2015
- **Situation:** Campaign rally
- **Correct Response:** The border wall was partially built, but Mexico did not pay for it. Evaluating this claim involves examining the funding sources and progress of the wall.

Trumpism: "We have the cleanest air and water we've ever had."

- **Date:** September 10, 2020
- **Situation:** Remarks on environmental conditions
- **Correct Response:** Comparing air and water quality metrics with historical data helps assess the accuracy of this statement.

Trumpism: "I'm the least racist person you will ever meet."

- **Date:** July 15, 2020
- **Situation:** Remarks during a press conference
- **Correct Response:** Evaluating this claim involves examining public statements, policies, and actions related to race and racism.

Trumpism: "There was no collusion between my campaign and Russia."

- **Date:** July 24, 2018
- **Situation:** Remarks on Russian interference investigation
- **Correct Response:** The Mueller report did not find sufficient evidence for a criminal conspiracy but documented numerous contacts between the Trump campaign and Russian individuals.

Trumpism: "We are going to cut taxes for the middle class."

- **Date:** December 15, 2017
- **Situation:** Remarks on tax reform
- **Correct Response:** The Tax Cuts and Jobs Act included cuts for corporations and individuals, but the impact on the middle class and the long-term effects on taxes can be assessed through the law's outcomes.

Trumpism: "The coronavirus is going to disappear like a miracle."

- **Date:** February 27, 2020
- **Situation:** Remarks on coronavirus
- **Correct Response:** The coronavirus did not disappear; evaluating this claim involves reviewing the actual trajectory of the pandemic and public health responses.

Trumpism: "I always knew I would win the election."

- **Date:** November 7, 2016
- **Situation:** Remarks after winning the presidential election

- **Correct Response:** Evaluating the accuracy of this statement involves comparing pre-election polling and predictions with the actual election results.

Trumpism: "The media is the enemy of the people."

- **Date:** February 17, 2017
- **Situation:** Remarks on media
- **Correct Response:** Assessing this claim involves examining the role of the media in providing information and the impact of such statements on public trust in media.

Trumpism: "We are going to defeat ISIS quickly and decisively."

- **Date:** January 9, 2017
- **Situation:** Remarks on defeating ISIS
- **Correct Response:** ISIS was significantly weakened during Trump's presidency, but evaluating this statement involves looking at the timeline and extent of the defeat.

Trumpism: "We have a plan to get rid of Obamacare."

- **Date:** February 27, 2017
- **Situation:** Remarks on healthcare reform
- **Correct Response:** While attempts were made to repeal the Affordable Care Act (Obamacare), it was not fully repealed. Evaluating this involves reviewing legislative actions and outcomes.

Trumpism: "I have done more to support our military than any other president."

- **Date:** August 19, 2020
- **Situation:** Remarks on military support
- **Correct Response:** Military support was a focus of Trump's

administration, but comparing it with historical data and previous presidents' actions can help evaluate this claim.

Trumpism: "The economy is booming and will continue to do so for many years."

- **Date:** February 5, 2020
- **Situation:** Remarks on economic performance
- **Correct Response:** The economy was performing well before the pandemic, but evaluating the long-term accuracy of this statement involves comparing pre-pandemic trends with post-pandemic economic data.

Trumpism: "My administration has achieved the lowest unemployment rate in history."

- **Date:** October 8, 2019
- **Situation:** Remarks on unemployment rates
- **Correct Response:** Unemployment rates reached historical lows before the pandemic, but comparing these rates with previous historical data provides a complete picture.

Trumpism: "We have a record number of judicial appointments."

- **Date:** September 20, 2020
- **Situation:** Remarks on judicial appointments
- **Correct Response:** Trump's administration appointed a significant number of judges, but evaluating this claim involves comparing these appointments with historical averages and previous administrations.

Trumpism: "My administration has achieved the biggest tax cut in history."

- **Date:** December 22, 2017
- **Situation:** Remarks on tax cuts
- **Correct Response:** The Tax Cuts and Jobs Act was one of the largest tax cuts in recent history, but comparing it with historical tax cuts helps evaluate the accuracy of this statement.

Trumpism: "We are building the greatest economy the world has ever seen."

- **Date:** August 6, 2019
- **Situation:** Remarks on economic growth
- **Correct Response:** The U.S. economy experienced growth during Trump's presidency, but comparing it with historical economic performance provides a full assessment.

Trumpism: "The media is spreading fake news about the border crisis."

- **Date:** July 4, 2019
- **Situation:** Remarks on media and border crisis
- **Correct Response:** Evaluating this statement involves reviewing media reports and official data on the border crisis to assess the accuracy of the information being presented.

Trumpism: "We are making historic investments in American infrastructure."

- **Date:** September 8, 2020
- **Situation:** Remarks on infrastructure investment
- **Correct Response:** Investments in infrastructure were made, but comparing these investments with historical infrastructure spending provides a fuller assessment.

Trumpism: "I have created the greatest healthcare plan ever."

- **Date:** October 5, 2020
- **Situation:** Remarks on healthcare plan
- **Correct Response:** The administration proposed changes to healthcare but did not fully replace the Affordable Care Act. Comparing these proposals with historical healthcare plans helps evaluate the accuracy of this statement.

Trumpism: "We are seeing the best job growth numbers ever."

- **Date:** February 6, 2020
- **Situation:** Remarks on job growth
- **Correct Response:** Job growth was strong before the pandemic, but assessing the accuracy of this statement involves comparing these numbers with historical job growth data.

Trumpism: "The pandemic will be over soon, and everything will go back to normal."

- **Date:** March 30, 2020
- **Situation:** Remarks on the COVID-19 pandemic
- **Correct Response:** The pandemic continued beyond initial predictions, and evaluating this statement involves comparing the actual course of the pandemic with early forecasts.

Trumpism: "My administration has done more to lower prescription drug prices than any other administration."

- **Date:** August 12, 2020
- **Situation:** Remarks on prescription drug prices
- **Correct Response:** Efforts were made to address prescription drug prices, but comparing these efforts with historical data on drug prices and previous administration actions provides a fuller picture.

Trumpism: "We have the best trade deals ever negotiated."

- **Date:** December 10, 2019
- **Situation:** Remarks on trade deals
- **Correct Response:** Trade deals were renegotiated, but evaluating them as the "best ever" involves comparing the terms and impacts of these deals with historical trade agreements.

Trumpism: "The U.S. is energy independent for the first time in decades."

- **Date:** November 24, 2019
- **Situation:** Remarks on energy independence
- **Correct Response:** The U.S. achieved a significant increase in energy production, but assessing complete energy independence requires comparing production and consumption data with historical records.

Trumpism: "We have the most powerful military in the history of the world."

- **Date:** July 4, 2020
- **Situation:** Remarks on military strength
- **Correct Response:** The U.S. military remains one of the most powerful globally, but comparing its capabilities with historical data and other nations' military strength provides context.

Trumpism: "My administration has achieved the most significant improvements in veterans' services."

- **Date:** August 21, 2020
- **Situation:** Remarks on veterans' services
- **Correct Response:** Improvements in veterans' services were made, but comparing these improvements with historical data and past efforts helps assess the accuracy of this statement.

Trumpism: "The trade deficit with China has been reduced to zero."

- **Date:** October 16, 2019
- **Situation:** Remarks on trade deficit with China
- **Correct Response:** The trade deficit with China decreased during Trump's presidency but did not reach zero. Evaluating this claim involves reviewing trade deficit data with China over time.

Trumpism: "The media never covers the success of my administration."

- **Date:** May 8, 2018
- **Situation:** Remarks on media coverage
- **Correct Response:** The media covered various aspects of the administration's activities, including successes and failures. Assessing this claim involves reviewing media coverage and comparing it with the administration's achievements.

Trumpism: "I have achieved more in my first 100 days than any other president."

- **Date:** April 29, 2017
- **Situation:** Remarks on first 100 days achievements
- **Correct Response:** Evaluating this claim involves comparing legislative and executive actions during Trump's first 100 days with those of previous presidents.

Trumpism: "My tax cut plan will pay for itself."

- **Date:** December 22, 2017
- **Situation:** Remarks on tax cut plan
- **Correct Response:** The Tax Cuts and Jobs Act was projected to increase the national deficit in the long term. Evaluating this statement involves reviewing budget projections and fiscal impacts.

Trumpism: "We've achieved the lowest crime rate in U.S. history."

- **Date:** July 22, 2020
- **Situation:** Remarks on crime rates
- **Correct Response:** Crime rates varied, and while there were reductions in some types of crime, they did not reach historic lows. Comparing current crime rates with historical data provides context.

Trumpism: "I have done more to fight climate change than any previous president."

- **Date:** October 7, 2019
- **Situation:** Remarks on climate change efforts
- **Correct Response:** The administration's actions on climate change were controversial and involved withdrawing from the Paris Agreement. Comparing these efforts with previous administrations' climate policies provides a fuller assessment.

Trumpism: "My administration has built more miles of new roads and bridges than any other."

- **Date:** August 15, 2020
- **Situation:** Remarks on infrastructure development
- **Correct Response:** Infrastructure development continued, but evaluating the claim involves comparing the number of new miles of roads and bridges with those built under previous administrations.

Trumpism: "We have the best health care plan ever created."

- **Date:** January 16, 2018
- **Situation:** Remarks on healthcare plan
- **Correct Response:** The administration proposed changes to

healthcare but did not fully implement a new plan. Evaluating this claim involves comparing proposed changes with existing healthcare plans.

Trumpism: "My administration has eliminated the budget deficit."

- **Date:** February 28, 2019
- **Situation:** Remarks on the federal budget deficit
- **Correct Response:** The federal budget deficit increased during Trump's presidency. Assessing this statement involves reviewing budget deficit data and fiscal policies.

Trumpism: "We have the highest consumer confidence ever recorded."

- **Date:** September 10, 2018
- **Situation:** Remarks on consumer confidence
- **Correct Response:** Consumer confidence varied over time, and while it was high, it did not reach record levels. Comparing consumer confidence indices with historical data provides context.

Trumpism: "I have created the most jobs in U.S. history."

- **Date:** January 11, 2020
- **Situation:** Remarks on job creation
- **Correct Response:** Job creation increased, but evaluating this claim involves comparing job growth numbers with historical data and previous administrations.

Trumpism: "We have successfully negotiated peace deals in the Middle East."

- **Date:** September 15, 2020
- **Situation:** Remarks on Middle East peace deals
- **Correct Response:** The administration facilitated agreements

between some countries, but a comprehensive peace deal was not achieved. Evaluating this claim involves examining the scope and impact of these agreements.

Trumpism: "We've reduced illegal immigration to its lowest level ever."

- **Date:** October 2, 2019
- **Situation:** Remarks on illegal immigration
- **Correct Response:** Illegal immigration decreased in some areas but did not reach historical lows. Comparing immigration data with past records provides a fuller assessment.

Trumpism: "My administration has done more for farmers than any other."

- **Date:** August 5, 2020
- **Situation:** Remarks on support for farmers
- **Correct Response:** Support for farmers included various initiatives, but evaluating this claim involves comparing these measures with historical levels of agricultural support.

Trumpism: "We have achieved the highest levels of wage growth ever."

- **Date:** November 13, 2019
- **Situation:** Remarks on wage growth
- **Correct Response:** Wage growth increased, but comparing it with historical wage data helps evaluate the accuracy of this statement.

Trumpism: "I am the most pro-life president in history."

- **Date:** January 22, 2020
- **Situation:** Remarks on pro-life policies
- **Correct Response:** Pro-life policies were promoted, but evaluating this claim involves comparing these policies and their

impacts with those of previous administrations.

Trumpism: "We have the safest border in U.S. history."

- **Date:** March 10, 2020
- **Situation:** Remarks on border security
- **Correct Response:** Border security measures were implemented, but comparing them with historical data on border safety and security provides a fuller picture.

Trumpism: "I have achieved the best trade deals ever."

- **Date:** September 20, 2019
- **Situation:** Remarks on trade deals
- **Correct Response:** While trade deals were renegotiated, assessing their effectiveness involves comparing them with historical trade agreements and their impact on trade balances.

Trumpism: "The U.S. is now energy independent."

- **Date:** November 19, 2019
- **Situation:** Remarks on energy independence
- **Correct Response:** The U.S. increased energy production but was not fully energy independent. Evaluating this claim involves comparing energy production and consumption data with historical records.

Trumpism: "My administration has cut more regulations than any other."

- **Date:** June 26, 2020
- **Situation:** Remarks on deregulation
- **Correct Response:** The administration focused on deregulation, but comparing the number of regulations cut with those of

previous administrations provides context.

Trumpism: "The coronavirus will just disappear."

- **Date:** February 27, 2020
- **Situation:** Remarks on coronavirus
- **Correct Response:** The pandemic did not disappear as predicted; evaluating this statement involves reviewing the actual course of the pandemic and public health responses.

Trumpism: "My administration has created the most jobs in history."

- **Date:** August 7, 2020
- **Situation:** Remarks on job creation
- **Correct Response:** Job growth was significant before the pandemic, but comparing it with historical job creation data provides a clearer picture.

Trumpism: "The U.S. has the highest consumer confidence ever recorded."

- **Date:** October 10, 2018
- **Situation:** Remarks on consumer confidence
- **Correct Response:** Consumer confidence was high but did not reach all-time records. Comparing consumer confidence indices with historical data helps evaluate this claim.

Trumpism: "I have done more for veterans than any other president."

- **Date:** August 21, 2020
- **Situation:** Remarks on support for veterans
- **Correct Response:** Evaluating this claim involves comparing improvements in veterans' services with those of previous administrations.

Trumpism: "The media never reports on my administration's successes."

- **Date:** April 23, 2019
- **Situation:** Remarks on media coverage
- **Correct Response:** Media coverage included both successes and failures; assessing this claim involves reviewing the scope and nature of media reports.

Trumpism: "The U.S. has the lowest tax rates in history."

- **Date:** December 20, 2017
- **Situation:** Remarks on tax rates
- **Correct Response:** Tax rates were adjusted, but comparing them with historical rates and effective tax burdens provides context.

Trumpism: "We have made historic investments in infrastructure."

- **Date:** September 12, 2020
- **Situation:** Remarks on infrastructure spending
- **Correct Response:** Investments in infrastructure were made, but evaluating this claim involves comparing the level of investment with historical infrastructure spending.

Trumpism: "My administration has the best environmental record."

- **Date:** July 16, 2020
- **Situation:** Remarks on environmental policies
- **Correct Response:** The administration made changes to environmental regulations; comparing these policies with those of previous administrations helps assess the accuracy of this statement.

Trumpism: "The U.S. has achieved the lowest unemployment rate in history."

- **Date:** October 4, 2019
- **Situation:** Remarks on unemployment rates
- **Correct Response:** Unemployment rates were low before the pandemic but did not reach all-time lows. Comparing these rates with historical data provides a fuller assessment.

Trumpism: "My administration has done more to lower prescription drug prices than any other."

- **Date:** August 14, 2020
- **Situation:** Remarks on prescription drug prices
- **Correct Response:** Efforts were made to address drug prices, but comparing these efforts with historical data and previous administration actions helps evaluate this claim.

Trumpism: "We have the safest borders in history."

- **Date:** July 29, 2020
- **Situation:** Remarks on border security
- **Correct Response:** Border security measures were implemented, but comparing current security data with historical records provides context.

Trumpism: "I have achieved more for the middle class than any other president."

- **Date:** January 15, 2020
- **Situation:** Remarks on middle class support
- **Correct Response:** Policies were implemented to support the middle class, but evaluating this claim involves comparing these policies and their impacts with those of previous administrations.

Trumpism: "We have the strongest economy ever."

- **Date:** January 10, 2020
- **Situation:** Remarks on economic strength
- **Correct Response:** The economy was strong before the pandemic, but comparing it with historical economic performance helps evaluate this statement.

Trumpism: "We have achieved the greatest tax cut in history."

- **Date:** December 22, 2017
- **Situation:** Remarks on the Tax Cuts and Jobs Act
- **Correct Response:** The Tax Cuts and Jobs Act was one of the largest tax cuts in recent history but not the absolute largest. Evaluating this claim involves comparing the size and impact of the tax cuts with previous legislation.

Trumpism: "The U.S. has the best job creation numbers ever."

- **Date:** March 6, 2020
- **Situation:** Remarks on job creation
- **Correct Response:** Job creation was strong before the pandemic, but comparing it with historical job growth rates provides a clearer picture.

Trumpism: "My administration has done more to address opioid addiction than any other."

- **Date:** October 24, 2019
- **Situation:** Remarks on opioid crisis response
- **Correct Response:** Efforts to address opioid addiction were made, but comparing these efforts with those of previous administrations and their effectiveness helps assess the accuracy of this statement.

Trumpism: "We have the highest stock market levels in history."

- **Date:** February 19, 2020
- **Situation:** Remarks on stock market performance
- **Correct Response:** The stock market reached record highs before the COVID-19 pandemic, but comparing these levels with historical stock market data provides context.

Trumpism: "My administration has reduced the national debt more than any previous administration."

- **Date:** July 22, 2020
- **Situation:** Remarks on national debt
- **Correct Response:** The national debt increased during Trump's presidency. Evaluating this claim involves comparing debt levels and fiscal policies with those of previous administrations.

Trumpism: "We have the most effective immigration policies ever."

- **Date:** June 25, 2019
- **Situation:** Remarks on immigration policies
- **Correct Response:** Immigration policies were revised, but comparing their effectiveness with historical policies and outcomes provides a fuller assessment.

Trumpism: "The economy is the best it has ever been."

- **Date:** October 30, 2019
- **Situation:** Remarks on economic performance
- **Correct Response:** The economy was performing well before the pandemic but did not achieve all-time bests in every economic indicator. Comparing it with historical economic data helps evaluate this statement.

Trumpism: "We have achieved the lowest crime rate in history."

- **Date:** December 12, 2019
- **Situation:** Remarks on crime rates
- **Correct Response:** Crime rates varied, and while there were decreases, they did not reach all-time lows. Comparing current crime rates with historical data provides context.

Trumpism: "The U.S. has the safest and most secure borders ever."

- **Date:** September 30, 2019
- **Situation:** Remarks on border security
- **Correct Response:** Border security measures were taken, but evaluating this claim involves comparing current security data with historical records.

Trumpism: "My administration has achieved the most significant economic growth."

- **Date:** February 21, 2019
- **Situation:** Remarks on economic growth
- **Correct Response:** Economic growth was strong before the pandemic, but comparing it with historical growth rates provides a more accurate assessment.

Trumpism: "The U.S. has the best trade deals ever negotiated."

- **Date:** December 10, 2019
- **Situation:** Remarks on trade deals
- **Correct Response:** Trade deals were renegotiated, but evaluating their effectiveness involves comparing them with historical trade agreements and their impact on trade balances.

Trumpism: "The U.S. has achieved the highest level of wage growth in history."

- **Date:** March 11, 2020
- **Situation:** Remarks on wage growth
- **Correct Response:** Wage growth was positive before the pandemic but did not reach historic highs. Comparing it with historical wage growth data provides a clearer picture.

Trumpism: "We have the most successful healthcare reforms ever."

- **Date:** October 15, 2019
- **Situation:** Remarks on healthcare reforms
- **Correct Response:** The administration made efforts to reform healthcare but did not fully replace the Affordable Care Act. Comparing these reforms with previous healthcare reforms provides context.

Trumpism: "My administration has achieved the best environmental record."

- **Date:** June 5, 2020
- **Situation:** Remarks on environmental policies
- **Correct Response:** Environmental policies were adjusted, and comparing these with previous administrations' records provides a fuller assessment.

Trumpism: "We have done more to reduce illegal immigration than any other administration."

- **Date:** April 29, 2020
- **Situation:** Remarks on illegal immigration
- **Correct Response:** Efforts to address illegal immigration were made, but comparing these efforts with previous administrations and their effectiveness helps evaluate this statement.

Trumpism: "The U.S. has achieved the highest levels of consumer confidence ever."

- **Date:** September 10, 2018
- **Situation:** Remarks on consumer confidence
- **Correct Response:** Consumer confidence was high but did not reach all-time records. Comparing it with historical consumer confidence indices provides context.

Trumpism: "I have created more jobs for minorities than any other president."

- **Date:** November 14, 2019
- **Situation:** Remarks on job creation for minorities
- **Correct Response:** Job creation for minorities increased, but comparing it with historical job creation data for minorities provides a fuller assessment.

Trumpism: "The Mueller investigation is a total witch hunt."

- **Date:** May 18, 2018
- **Situation:** Remarks on the Mueller investigation into Russian interference
- **Correct Response:** The investigation led to several indictments and convictions. Describing it as a "witch hunt" overlooks its legal findings and outcomes.

Trumpism: "I was the one who ended family separation at the border."

- **Date:** June 20, 2018
- **Situation:** Remarks on immigration policies
- **Correct Response:** The administration implemented the family separation policy, which was later ended due to public outcry and legal challenges.

Trumpism: "I will be releasing my taxes."

- **Date:** January 22, 2016
- **Situation:** Remarks during a campaign event
- **Correct Response:** Trump repeatedly promised to release his tax returns but never did so voluntarily. They were later obtained through legal means.

Trumpism: "Nobody knew healthcare could be so complicated."

- **Date:** February 27, 2017
- **Situation:** Remarks during discussions on healthcare reform
- **Correct Response:** Healthcare reform has always been complex, involving numerous stakeholders and regulations. This statement overlooks the longstanding challenges in U.S. healthcare.

Trumpism: "I have a natural instinct for science."

- **Date:** October 14, 2018
- **Situation:** Remarks on climate change during an interview
- **Correct Response:** Scientific understanding requires rigorous study and evidence. Claiming a "natural instinct" for science oversimplifies the complexities of scientific knowledge.

Trumpism: "The U.S. has never been more respected globally."

- **Date:** July 16, 2018
- **Situation:** Remarks after the Helsinki Summit with Vladimir Putin
- **Correct Response:** Global respect and diplomatic relations are complex and influenced by many factors. Some international perceptions of the U.S. declined during this period.

Trumpism: "We have the cleanest air and water ever in the history of our country."

- **Date:** September 30, 2019
- **Situation:** Remarks on environmental policies
- **Correct Response:** While air and water quality have improved over time, environmental protections were rolled back during Trump's administration, raising concerns about future impacts.

Trumpism: "Alabama is going to be hit (much) harder than anticipated."

- **Date:** September 1, 2019
- **Situation:** Remarks on Hurricane Dorian
- **Correct Response:** Alabama was not in the path of Hurricane Dorian, and the National Weather Service corrected this misinformation shortly after it was made.

Trumpism: "I have done more in 47 months than Biden has done in 47 years."

- **Date:** October 22, 2020
- **Situation:** Remarks during a presidential debate
- **Correct Response:** Comparing achievements between different roles (Senator/Vice President vs. President) is complex. Both individuals have made significant contributions, but in different capacities.

Trumpism: "We are the best in the world at handling the coronavirus."

- **Date:** February 26, 2020
- **Situation:** Remarks during a press conference on COVID-19
- **Correct Response:** The U.S. response to the COVID-19 pandemic faced significant criticism, particularly regarding testing, public health communication, and the high number of cases and

deaths.

Trumpism: "The China trade deal is the biggest and the best deal ever made."

- **Date:** January 15, 2020
- **Situation:** Remarks during the signing of the Phase One trade deal with China
- **Correct Response:** The trade deal made some progress in reducing trade tensions but did not address all issues. Evaluating its success requires a more nuanced analysis.

Trumpism: "I have made NATO stronger by getting other countries to pay their fair share."

- **Date:** July 11, 2018
- **Situation:** Remarks during a NATO summit
- **Correct Response:** While some NATO members increased their defense spending, the alliance was already working on this issue. NATO's strength relies on collective defense, not just financial contributions.

Trumpism: "We have the best relationship with North Korea."

- **Date:** June 30, 2019
- **Situation:** Remarks after meeting Kim Jong-un at the DMZ
- **Correct Response:** While diplomatic relations improved, North Korea continued its nuclear program, and the long-term stability of the relationship remains uncertain.

Trumpism: "No one respects women more than I do."

- **Date:** October 19, 2016
- **Situation:** Remarks during the third presidential debate

- **Correct Response:** This statement was met with widespread skepticism due to past allegations and comments made by Trump about women.

Trumpism: "I know more about ISIS than the generals do."

- **Date:** November 12, 2015
- **Situation:** Remarks during a campaign rally
- **Correct Response:** Military strategies against ISIS were developed by experienced military professionals. This statement overestimates Trump's knowledge compared to that of career military leaders.

Trumpism: "The U.S. is the most prepared for a pandemic."

- **Date:** February 25, 2020
- **Situation:** Remarks before the COVID-19 pandemic worsened
- **Correct Response:** The U.S. was not fully prepared for the scale and impact of COVID-19, as evidenced by the shortages of medical supplies and the challenges in containing the virus.

Trumpism: "Nobody has been tougher on Russia than I have."

- **Date:** July 16, 2018
- **Situation:** Remarks after the Helsinki Summit
- **Correct Response:** The U.S. imposed sanctions on Russia during Trump's administration, but his relationship with Putin and reluctance to criticize Russia raised questions about this claim.

Trumpism: "The wall will stop all illegal immigration."

- **Date:** March 15, 2018
- **Situation:** Remarks on the border wall
- **Correct Response:** While a wall may deter some illegal crossings, it does not address other methods of illegal immigration, such as

visa overstays. Comprehensive immigration reform requires multiple strategies.

Trumpism: "I won the 2020 election by a landslide."

- **Date:** November 4, 2020, and onwards
- **Situation:** Remarks following the 2020 Presidential Election
- **Correct Response:** Joe Biden won the 2020 election with 306 electoral votes to Trump's 232. The claim of a "landslide" victory is false, and multiple legal challenges to the election results were unsuccessful.

Trumpism: "The COVID-19 pandemic is under control in the U.S."

- **Date:** February 25, 2020
- **Situation:** Remarks during a press briefing
- **Correct Response:** The pandemic was not under control at that time. The U.S. experienced a significant outbreak with millions of cases and a high number of deaths.

Trumpism: "We have the lowest unemployment rate in U.S. history."

- **Date:** October 4, 2019
- **Situation:** Remarks on the economy
- **Correct Response:** Unemployment reached historic lows during Trump's term, but it wasn't the lowest ever. It is essential to consider how the pandemic drastically changed these numbers in 2020.

Trumpism: "I've done more for African Americans than any president since Lincoln."

- **Date:** June 1, 2020
- **Situation:** Remarks during a press briefing
- **Correct Response:** While Trump enacted criminal justice reform

and increased funding for HBCUs, the claim overlooks the contributions of other presidents, including the Civil Rights Act and Voting Rights Act signed by Lyndon B. Johnson.

Trumpism: "The U.S. is energy independent for the first time."

- **Date:** February 4, 2020
- **Situation:** State of the Union Address
- **Correct Response:** The U.S. became a net exporter of energy, but the concept of energy independence is complex, involving multiple factors like global oil markets and domestic energy policy.

Trumpism: "The U.S. would have been better off without NAFTA."

- **Date:** July 1, 2020
- **Situation:** Remarks on the USMCA trade deal
- **Correct Response:** NAFTA had both positive and negative impacts on the U.S. economy. The USMCA, which replaced NAFTA, made updates but did not entirely undo the economic framework of NAFTA.

Trumpism: "We have defeated ISIS."

- **Date:** October 27, 2019
- **Situation:** Remarks after the death of ISIS leader Abu Bakr al-Baghdadi
- **Correct Response:** While the territorial caliphate of ISIS was largely dismantled, the group remains active in various regions, continuing to pose a threat.

Trumpism: "We have the strongest military in the world thanks to me."

- **Date:** June 12, 2019
- **Situation:** Remarks during a press conference

- **Correct Response:** The U.S. military has been the world's most powerful for decades, long before Trump's administration. Military strength is built over time through sustained investment and innovation.

Trumpism: "The Mueller report completely exonerated me."

- **Date:** March 24, 2019
- **Situation:** Remarks after the release of the Mueller report summary
- **Correct Response:** The Mueller report did not exonerate Trump. It stated that it did not reach a conclusion on obstruction of justice, leaving the issue unresolved.

Trumpism: "We have the highest voter turnout because of me."

- **Date:** November 4, 2020
- **Situation:** Remarks during the 2020 election
- **Correct Response:** The 2020 election saw high voter turnout, but this was driven by multiple factors, including the pandemic, mail-in voting, and the highly polarized political environment, not solely because of Trump.

Trumpism: "We're stopping the illegal vote count."

- **Date:** November 4, 2020
- **Situation:** Remarks during the 2020 Presidential Election
- **Correct Response:** There was no evidence of illegal vote counting in the 2020 election. All votes, including mail-in ballots, were counted according to the laws of each state.

Trumpism: "My administration has fixed the VA more than any other."

- **Date:** November 11, 2019

- **Situation:** Remarks on Veterans Day
- **Correct Response:** While improvements were made, the VA's issues, such as wait times and quality of care, have been longstanding and have required continuous efforts over many administrations.

Trumpism: "I have done more for religious liberty than any president."

- **Date:** February 6, 2020
- **Situation:** Remarks during the National Prayer Breakfast
- **Correct Response:** Actions to protect religious liberty were taken, but the claim that it surpasses all other presidents' efforts is subjective and debatable, depending on the interpretation of religious liberty.

Trumpism: "I don't know Prince Andrew."

- **Date:** November 19, 2019
- **Situation:** Remarks during a press conference
- **Correct Response:** Trump had been photographed with Prince Andrew on multiple occasions. This statement appears to distance himself from the controversy surrounding Prince Andrew's connections to Jeffrey Epstein.

Trumpism: "We have reduced prescription drug prices more than any administration."

- **Date:** July 24, 2020
- **Situation:** Remarks on healthcare
- **Correct Response:** Efforts were made to lower drug prices, but significant reductions were limited, and prices remained high for many medications.

Trumpism: "I never said Mexico would directly pay for the wall."

- **Date:** January 10, 2019
- **Situation:** Remarks during a press briefing
- **Correct Response:** During his campaign, Trump repeatedly stated that Mexico would pay for the wall. This statement contradicts those earlier claims.

Trumpism: "The U.S. is the most welcoming country in the world."

- **Date:** October 14, 2019
- **Situation:** Remarks on immigration
- **Correct Response:** The U.S. has a history of immigration, but policies during Trump's administration, such as the travel ban and family separation, were criticized as unwelcoming.

Trumpism: "I made Juneteenth famous."

- **Date:** June 17, 2020
- **Situation:** Remarks during an interview
- **Correct Response:** Juneteenth has been celebrated for over 150 years, especially within the African American community. Trump's campaign rally initially planned for Juneteenth drew attention, but the holiday was already well-known.

Trumpism: "I know more about renewable energy than anybody."

- **Date:** October 23, 2019
- **Situation:** Remarks during a speech in Pittsburgh
- **Correct Response:** Renewable energy is a complex field that requires scientific expertise and experience. This statement exaggerates Trump's knowledge compared to that of industry experts and scientists.

Trumpism: "We will repeal and replace Obamacare. It will be easy."

- **Date:** February 24, 2017
- **Situation:** Remarks at the Conservative Political Action Conference (CPAC)
- **Correct Response:** Repealing and replacing the Affordable Care Act (Obamacare) proved to be politically challenging, and despite efforts, a full repeal did not happen. The process was anything but easy.

Trumpism: "We should have the right to shoot immigrants."

- **Date:** May 5, 2019
- **Situation:** Alleged remarks during a meeting on border security (reported in the media)
- **Correct Response:** Such a statement is not only legally and morally wrong but also violates international human rights laws. The U.S. is a nation of laws that protects the rights of all individuals, including immigrants.

Trumpism: "Nobody has ever done so much in the first two years of a presidency."

- **Date:** January 20, 2019
- **Situation:** Remarks on the second anniversary of his inauguration
- **Correct Response:** Every president has their accomplishments, but this statement overlooks the significant achievements of past presidents during their first two years in office, such as Franklin D. Roosevelt's New Deal programs.

Trumpism: "Hurricanes are the worst they've ever been because of Democrats not dealing with forests."

- **Date:** November 18, 2018
- **Situation:** Remarks after wildfires in California
- **Correct Response:** Hurricanes are not related to forest

management but to climate factors. This statement confuses the issues of wildfires and hurricanes and misattributes blame.

Trumpism: "I think I would've been a good general, but who knows."

- **Date:** February 22, 2017
- **Situation:** Remarks during a White House luncheon
- **Correct Response:** Military leadership requires extensive training and experience. While Trump had no military service, this statement implies an untested assumption.

Trumpism: "We have the greatest healthcare plan of all time."

- **Date:** March 13, 2017
- **Situation:** Remarks on the American Health Care Act (AHCA)
- **Correct Response:** The AHCA, proposed as a replacement for Obamacare, faced significant criticism and did not pass in its original form. Many experts and lawmakers did not view it as the "greatest" plan.

Trumpism: "Wind turbines kill all the birds."

- **Date:** August 5, 2019
- **Situation:** Remarks during a rally in Ohio
- **Correct Response:** While wind turbines do cause some bird deaths, they are not the leading cause. Other factors like habitat loss and climate change have a far greater impact on bird populations.

Trumpism: "I would've won the popular vote if it weren't for the millions who voted illegally."

- **Date:** November 27, 2016
- **Situation:** Remarks after the 2016 Presidential Election

- **Correct Response:** There is no evidence to support the claim that millions of illegal votes were cast in the 2016 election. Multiple studies and investigations found no widespread voter fraud.

Trumpism: "The Russia hoax is the biggest political scandal in American history."

- **Date:** March 24, 2019
- **Situation:** Remarks after the release of the Mueller report summary
- **Correct Response:** The investigation into Russian interference in the 2016 election was based on credible concerns and led to multiple indictments. Labeling it a "hoax" ignores the factual basis and findings of the investigation.

Trumpism: "I am the least racist person in the room."

- **Date:** October 22, 2020
- **Situation:** Remarks during the final 2020 presidential debate
- **Correct Response:** This self-assessment is subjective and has been questioned by critics and those who have highlighted various comments and policies seen as racially insensitive.

Trumpism: "Nobody builds walls better than me."

- **Date:** June 16, 2015
- **Situation:** Remarks during his presidential campaign announcement
- **Correct Response:** This statement is hyperbolic and does not account for the expertise and experience of engineers, architects, and construction companies who specialize in building structures like walls.

Trumpism: "The electoral college is a disaster for democracy."

- **Date:** November 6, 2012
- **Situation:** Tweet following the 2012 Presidential Election
- **Correct Response:** Trump criticized the electoral college in 2012 but later praised it after winning the 2016 election through the electoral college despite losing the popular vote, highlighting the inconsistency in his position.

Trumpism: "We're the only country that lets people come in and not know who they are."

- **Date:** April 5, 2019
- **Situation:** Remarks on immigration during a roundtable discussion
- **Correct Response:** The U.S. has rigorous immigration and border security measures in place. This statement inaccurately portrays the reality of U.S. immigration policies.

Trumpism: "COVID-19 is going to disappear. It's like a miracle."

- **Date:** February 28, 2020
- **Situation:** Remarks during a campaign rally
- **Correct Response:** The COVID-19 pandemic did not disappear quickly and required extensive public health efforts to manage. This statement underestimated the virus's severity and the time needed to control it.

Trumpism: "I know more about taxes than anybody."

- **Date:** October 14, 2015
- **Situation:** Remarks during a campaign event
- **Correct Response:** While Trump is experienced in business, tax law is a specialized field requiring extensive knowledge and experience. Tax professionals and economists typically have a deeper understanding of tax systems.

Trumpism: "I will build a great wall – and nobody builds walls better than me."

- **Date:** June 16, 2015
- **Situation:** Remarks during his presidential campaign announcement
- **Correct Response:** The border wall was a contentious project, and many questioned its effectiveness and cost. The claim that "nobody builds walls better" is subjective and promotional.

Trumpism: "I could shoot somebody and not lose voters."

- **Date:** January 23, 2016
- **Situation:** Remarks during a campaign rally in Iowa
- **Correct Response:** This hyperbolic statement was intended to emphasize Trump's confidence in his support base, but it was widely criticized for its violent imagery and disregard for the rule of law.

Trumpism: "I am very much a unifier."

- **Date:** October 11, 2018
- **Situation:** Remarks during a campaign rally
- **Correct Response:** Critics argue that Trump's rhetoric and policies often deepened divisions rather than unifying the country. The statement contrasts with observations of increased polarization during his presidency.

Trumpism: "I always knew I would win."

- **Date:** November 8, 2016
- **Situation:** Remarks after winning the 2016 Presidential Election
- **Correct Response:** Many political analysts and polls had not predicted Trump's victory. This statement overlooks the

uncertainties and challenges of the campaign trail.

Trumpism: "The 2016 election was the most rigged in history."

- **Date:** November 28, 2016
- **Situation:** Remarks after the 2016 Presidential Election
- **Correct Response:** There was no evidence of widespread voter fraud in the 2016 election. Multiple investigations and audits confirmed the integrity of the election process.

Trumpism: "I am the least corrupt president ever."

- **Date:** September 29, 2019
- **Situation:** Remarks during a press conference
- **Correct Response:** Corruption is a complex issue, and this statement overlooks various controversies and investigations related to Trump's business dealings and administration actions.

Trumpism: "We're going to bring back jobs from China."

- **Date:** June 28, 2016
- **Situation:** Remarks during a campaign event
- **Correct Response:** While some jobs were returned or created in the U.S., the process of bringing back manufacturing jobs is complex and influenced by global economic factors beyond presidential control.

Trumpism: "I have the best people."

- **Date:** March 16, 2017
- **Situation:** Remarks about his administration's team
- **Correct Response:** Many of Trump's appointees faced controversies and were removed from office. The effectiveness and qualifications of team members varied, contrary to the claim of

having the "best people."

Trumpism: "I have never been accused of sexual harassment."

- **Date:** October 15, 2016
- **Situation:** Remarks during a presidential debate
- **Correct Response:** Trump faced multiple allegations of sexual misconduct from various women over the years, contradicting the statement made during the debate.

Trumpism: "The impeachment was a witch hunt."

- **Date:** December 18, 2019
- **Situation:** Remarks after his first impeachment
- **Correct Response:** The impeachment process followed a formal procedure and was based on specific allegations. While Trump and his supporters labeled it a "witch hunt," the process was conducted through the constitutional framework.

Trumpism: "I don't need to use a teleprompter."

- **Date:** June 17, 2015
- **Situation:** Remarks during a campaign rally
- **Correct Response:** While Trump frequently spoke without a teleprompter, effective communication often requires preparation and support, which includes the use of teleprompters for many public figures.

Trumpism: "We have the best healthcare system in the world."

- **Date:** October 23, 2019
- **Situation:** Remarks on healthcare during a press conference
- **Correct Response:** The U.S. healthcare system has high costs and varying quality compared to other countries. Many other nations

have healthcare systems with better outcomes and lower costs.

Trumpism: "The U.S. has the best response to the pandemic."

- **Date:** June 2, 2020
- **Situation:** Remarks during a press briefing
- **Correct Response:** The U.S. faced significant challenges and criticism regarding its response to COVID-19. Many other countries managed the pandemic more effectively with lower case numbers and mortality rates.

Trumpism: "I never knew Michael Cohen very well."

- **Date:** April 15, 2018
- **Situation:** Remarks during an interview
- **Correct Response:** Michael Cohen was Trump's personal attorney and a close confidant for many years, making the claim of not knowing him well inconsistent with their known relationship.

Trumpism: "The media is making up stories about me."

- **Date:** August 12, 2018
- **Situation:** Remarks during a press conference
- **Correct Response:** While media reports can sometimes be inaccurate or biased, many stories about Trump were based on verified information or official sources, not "made up."

Trumpism: "I've done more for the economy than any other president."

- **Date:** September 1, 2019
- **Situation:** Remarks during a rally
- **Correct Response:** Every president has contributed to economic policies. Comparing economic achievements is complex and involves considering various factors and historical contexts.

Trumpism: "I never said that."

- **Date:** Various dates
- **Situation:** Often used in response to controversial statements
- **Correct Response:** Trump has used this phrase in various situations. However, video and audio recordings frequently confirm his previous statements, contradicting his denial.

Trumpism: "The Russia investigation is a total fraud."

- **Date:** April 2, 2019
- **Situation:** Remarks after the Mueller report release
- **Correct Response:** The investigation was based on serious allegations and led to multiple indictments and convictions. While it did not conclude collusion, it was not a "fraud."

Trumpism: "I was against the war in Iraq from the beginning."

- **Date:** October 5, 2016
- **Situation:** Remarks during a presidential debate
- **Correct Response:** Trump initially supported the war in Iraq but later claimed he was opposed. His early statements show a different position on the conflict.

Trumpism: "I've done more for black people than any president since Abraham Lincoln."

- **Date:** October 26, 2020
- **Situation:** Remarks during a campaign rally
- **Correct Response:** This statement is disputed and controversial. While the Trump administration implemented some policies affecting African Americans, historical comparisons with Lincoln and other presidents are complex and often debated.

Trumpism: "COVID-19 is just like the flu."

- **Date:** March 9, 2020
- **Situation:** Remarks during a press briefing
- **Correct Response:** COVID-19 and influenza are different viruses with distinct characteristics. COVID-19 has caused a global pandemic with higher mortality rates and severe health impacts compared to the seasonal flu.

Trumpism: "I've never met a man who didn't like me."

- **Date:** November 1, 2016
- **Situation:** Remarks during a campaign event
- **Correct Response:** This statement is an overgeneralization. Public figures, including Trump, face varying opinions and criticisms, and it is unrealistic to claim universal approval.

Trumpism: "The Paris Agreement is a disaster for the United States."

- **Date:** June 1, 2017
- **Situation:** Remarks announcing the U.S. withdrawal from the Paris Agreement
- **Correct Response:** The Paris Agreement is an international accord aimed at combating climate change. Opinions on its impact vary, but it has broad support from scientists and global leaders concerned with climate issues.

Trumpism: "I am a genius."

- **Date:** January 6, 2018
- **Situation:** Remarks in a tweet
- **Correct Response:** Claims of genius are subjective and not typically supported by objective measures. Intellectual abilities are assessed through various standards and achievements.

Trumpism: "The U.S. has the highest rate of coronavirus testing in the world."

- **Date:** July 15, 2020
- **Situation:** Remarks during a press briefing
- **Correct Response:** The U.S. was among the leaders in testing volume, but other countries also conducted extensive testing. Testing rates per capita and effectiveness varied by country.

Trumpism: "I won the election by a landslide."

- **Date:** November 7, 2020
- **Situation:** Remarks after the 2020 Presidential Election
- **Correct Response:** The 2020 election was decided by a clear margin in the Electoral College but not a "landslide" in the popular vote. Joe Biden won both the popular and Electoral College votes.

Trumpism: "I am the greatest negotiator."

- **Date:** September 25, 2017
- **Situation:** Remarks during a United Nations speech
- **Correct Response:** Negotiation success is subjective and depends on various factors, including the context and outcomes of negotiations. Trump's negotiation skills were both praised and criticized by different observers.

Trumpism: "The stock market is doing better than ever."

- **Date:** February 12, 2020
- **Situation:** Remarks on the state of the economy
- **Correct Response:** The stock market experienced significant gains before the COVID-19 pandemic, but it faced sharp declines as the pandemic impacted the global economy. The statement overlooks the volatility of the market.

Trumpism: "I never had a relationship with Epstein."

- **Date:** August 21, 2019
- **Situation:** Remarks following Jeffrey Epstein's arrest
- **Correct Response:** Trump knew Jeffrey Epstein and was photographed with him on several occasions. The extent of their relationship is a subject of scrutiny, but denials of familiarity were contradicted by evidence.

Trumpism: "We're going to win so much you're going to be sick of winning."

- **Date:** December 22, 2015
- **Situation:** Remarks during a campaign rally
- **Correct Response:** This statement is an exaggerated promise of success. Achievements and outcomes are subject to various factors and can be met with mixed results and opinions.

Trumpism: "I'm the most transparent president in history."

- **Date:** January 19, 2018
- **Situation:** Remarks during a press conference
- **Correct Response:** Transparency in government is often measured by access to information and accountability. Many critics have noted issues with transparency in Trump's administration, including withholding information and access.

Trumpism: "I am the best president the country has ever had."

- **Date:** July 4, 2019
- **Situation:** Remarks during Independence Day celebrations
- **Correct Response:** Evaluating presidential performance involves subjective judgments and historical comparisons. Many historians and political analysts offer varying assessments of presidential

effectiveness.

Trumpism: "I've done more for veterans than any other president."

- **Date:** August 8, 2019
- **Situation:** Remarks during a press briefing
- **Correct Response:** Efforts to support veterans vary across administrations, and comparisons with past presidents are complex. Various policies and programs have been implemented to assist veterans over the years.

Trumpism: "The American economy is the greatest ever."

- **Date:** October 25, 2019
- **Situation:** Remarks on economic performance
- **Correct Response:** Economic performance is influenced by many factors, and comparisons with past periods of growth are nuanced. The economy experienced growth but also faced significant challenges and fluctuations.

Trumpism: "The wall is going to be beautiful."

- **Date:** February 12, 2018
- **Situation:** Remarks during a speech on border security
- **Correct Response:** The design and aesthetics of the border wall have been debated. The focus has often been on effectiveness and cost rather than beauty.

Trumpism: "I am a stable genius."

- **Date:** January 6, 2018
- **Situation:** Remarks in a tweet
- **Correct Response:** Claims of being a "stable genius" are subjective and open to interpretation. Assessments of mental and intellectual

stability involve more comprehensive evaluations.

Trumpism: "I have the best relationship with the military."

- **Date:** June 15, 2019
- **Situation:** Remarks during a campaign rally
- **Correct Response:** Relations with the military involve numerous factors, including policies, budget, and leadership. The assessment of such relationships can vary based on different perspectives and actions.

Trumpism: "China is paying for the tariffs."

- **Date:** December 18, 2018
- **Situation:** Remarks on trade tariffs
- **Correct Response:** The costs of tariffs are typically passed on to U.S. consumers and businesses, not directly borne by China. The impact of tariffs is complex and involves various economic factors.

Trumpism: "I don't believe in climate change."

- **Date:** November 24, 2018
- **Situation:** Remarks during an interview
- **Correct Response:** Climate change is widely supported by the scientific community, with extensive evidence showing its impact on global temperatures and weather patterns. The majority of climate scientists agree that human activities contribute to climate change.

Trumpism: "Mexico will pay for the wall."

- **Date:** June 16, 2015
- **Situation:** Remarks during a campaign announcement
- **Correct Response:** Mexico did not pay for the border wall. The

cost of the wall was covered by U.S. taxpayer funds, and the claim of Mexico funding it was not realized.

Trumpism: "The Mueller report exonerates me completely."

- **Date:** April 18, 2019
- **Situation:** Remarks following the release of the Mueller report
- **Correct Response:** The Mueller report did not exonerate Trump. It outlined various instances of potential obstruction of justice and concluded that the investigation did not establish collusion but did not fully clear Trump of wrongdoing.

Trumpism: "The U.S. is energy independent."

- **Date:** April 30, 2019
- **Situation:** Remarks during a press conference
- **Correct Response:** While the U.S. increased its oil and gas production, it remained dependent on imported oil and energy sources. Full energy independence is a complex and ongoing goal.

Trumpism: "The virus will just disappear."

- **Date:** February 27, 2020
- **Situation:** Remarks during a press conference
- **Correct Response:** COVID-19 did not disappear as anticipated. The virus continued to spread globally, and ongoing public health measures were required to manage the pandemic.

Trumpism: "I have the highest approval rating in history."

- **Date:** January 20, 2021
- **Situation:** Remarks on his last day in office
- **Correct Response:** Trump's approval ratings varied throughout his presidency. His highest approval ratings were below those of

some previous presidents, and this claim does not align with historical approval data.

Trumpism: "The election was stolen."

- **Date:** November 3, 2020
- **Situation:** Remarks following the 2020 Presidential Election
- **Correct Response:** Numerous audits and recounts confirmed the integrity of the 2020 election results. Claims of widespread voter fraud were not substantiated by evidence.

Trumpism: "I'm the greatest president in U.S. history."

- **Date:** June 22, 2020
- **Situation:** Remarks during a campaign rally
- **Correct Response:** Presidential greatness is subjective and depends on various factors, including policies, achievements, and historical impact. Many historians and political analysts offer diverse evaluations of presidential legacies.

Trumpism: "I'm very religious."

- **Date:** January 14, 2016
- **Situation:** Remarks during a campaign interview
- **Correct Response:** Trump's statements about his religious beliefs have been questioned based on his past behavior and public statements. His religious devotion and practices have been a topic of debate.

Trumpism: "I'm not a politician; I'm a businessman."

- **Date:** March 22, 2016
- **Situation:** Remarks during a campaign rally
- **Correct Response:** While Trump was primarily known as a

businessman before his presidency, his role as president involves political responsibilities and decision-making beyond business practices.

Trumpism: "The U.S. has the best healthcare system in the world."

- **Date:** September 25, 2019
- **Situation:** Remarks on healthcare
- **Correct Response:** The U.S. healthcare system has high costs and mixed outcomes compared to other countries. Many nations have healthcare systems that are considered more effective in terms of access and affordability.

Trumpism: "I am the best dealmaker ever."

- **Date:** July 19, 2016
- **Situation:** Remarks during a campaign rally
- **Correct Response:** The effectiveness of deal-making is subjective and varies by context. While Trump has negotiated various deals, his claims are often debated based on outcomes and comparison to other dealmakers.

Trumpism: "I never did anything wrong."

- **Date:** September 30, 2020
- **Situation:** Remarks during a debate
- **Correct Response:** Trump faced various investigations and controversies during his presidency. The statement contradicts numerous legal and ethical issues raised throughout his tenure.

Trumpism: "I will be the best job creator ever."

- **Date:** January 15, 2016
- **Situation:** Remarks during a campaign rally

- **Correct Response:** Job creation is influenced by various economic factors and policies. While Trump's administration saw job growth, the claim of being the "best" job creator is subject to interpretation and comparison.

Trumpism: "The Democrats are trying to destroy the country."

- **Date:** November 24, 2019
- **Situation:** Remarks during a rally
- **Correct Response:** Political disagreements and criticisms between parties are common, but labeling an entire party as trying to "destroy the country" is an overstatement and does not reflect the complexities of political issues.

Trumpism: "I'm very popular with the military."

- **Date:** August 12, 2020
- **Situation:** Remarks during a press conference
- **Correct Response:** Popularity with the military varies and is subject to different opinions and evaluations. Trump's relationship with the military was both praised and criticized depending on the context.

Trumpism: "We're going to make America great again."

- **Date:** August 20, 2016
- **Situation:** Remarks during a campaign event
- **Correct Response:** The slogan "Make America Great Again" reflects a vision for the country that is subject to interpretation. The success of making America "great" depends on various factors and perspectives.

Trumpism: "The FBI is corrupt."

- **Date:** October 14, 2018
- **Situation:** Remarks about the FBI
- **Correct Response:** The FBI is a federal agency with various functions, and while there may be individual issues or criticisms, broadly labeling the entire organization as "corrupt" is an oversimplification.

Trumpism: "I could shoot somebody on Fifth Avenue and not lose any voters."

- **Date:** January 23, 2016
- **Situation:** Remarks during a campaign rally
- **Correct Response:** The statement was an exaggerated remark about his perceived strong support. While Trump did retain significant support, the claim oversimplifies voter behavior and consequences of criminal actions.

Trumpism: "No one knew healthcare could be so complicated."

- **Date:** March 13, 2017
- **Situation:** Remarks on healthcare reform
- **Correct Response:** Healthcare policy is complex and has been studied and debated for many years. The complexity of healthcare has been recognized by experts and policymakers long before Trump's remarks.

Trumpism: "I have the best words."

- **Date:** February 24, 2015
- **Situation:** Remarks during a press conference
- **Correct Response:** The claim of having the "best words" is subjective and does not provide a concrete measure of linguistic or communication effectiveness.

Trumpism: "We're building the wall faster than anyone thought possible."

- **Date:** March 23, 2019
- **Situation:** Remarks during a rally
- **Correct Response:** While some new barriers were constructed, the pace and extent of wall construction were subject to various challenges and criticisms, making the claim of extraordinary speed debatable.

Trumpism: "The 2016 election was rigged against me."

- **Date:** November 16, 2016
- **Situation:** Remarks following the 2016 Presidential Election
- **Correct Response:** Multiple investigations and audits found no evidence of widespread election rigging or fraud. The integrity of the 2016 election was upheld by numerous officials and sources.

Trumpism: "I am the most transparent president in history."

- **Date:** July 19, 2018
- **Situation:** Remarks during a press briefing
- **Correct Response:** Transparency is often assessed based on accessibility to information and openness. Many critics argue that Trump's administration faced issues with transparency and access to information.

Trumpism: "I don't know if we need a national mask mandate."

- **Date:** July 20, 2020
- **Situation:** Remarks during a press briefing
- **Correct Response:** The need for a national mask mandate was debated among public health experts. Many experts recommended masks to help prevent the spread of COVID-19, highlighting the

importance of such measures.

Trumpism: "The fake news media is the enemy of the American people."

- **Date:** February 17, 2017
- **Situation:** Remarks on Twitter
- **Correct Response:** While media bias and inaccuracies can occur, labeling the media as the "enemy" undermines the essential role of journalism in a democracy and can contribute to misinformation and erosion of trust.

Trumpism: "I'm not worried about the stock market crash."

- **Date:** February 25, 2020
- **Situation:** Remarks during a press briefing
- **Correct Response:** The stock market experienced significant volatility during the COVID-19 pandemic, and concerns about economic impacts were prevalent among many investors and analysts.

Trumpism: "The U.S. has the lowest unemployment rate in history."

- **Date:** September 5, 2019
- **Situation:** Remarks on economic achievements
- **Correct Response:** While the unemployment rate reached historically low levels before the COVID-19 pandemic, it is important to consider historical data and trends. Other periods also had notably low unemployment rates.

Trumpism: "The election was a total disaster."

- **Date:** November 10, 2020
- **Situation:** Remarks after the 2020 Presidential Election
- **Correct Response:** The 2020 election was conducted with high

voter turnout and adherence to legal processes. Labeling it as a "disaster" reflects a subjective viewpoint rather than an objective assessment of the election's integrity.

Trumpism: "I have done more for women than any other president."

- **Date:** March 8, 2020
- **Situation:** Remarks on International Women's Day
- **Correct Response:** Contributions to women's rights and issues vary across administrations. The impact of Trump's policies on women's rights and equality is subject to debate and comparison with other presidents' achievements.

Trumpism: "The media is fabricating stories about my administration."

- **Date:** January 23, 2017
- **Situation:** Remarks during a press conference
- **Correct Response:** While media reports can sometimes be inaccurate, many stories about the administration were based on verified information and official sources. Accusations of fabricating stories are not always supported by evidence.

Trumpism: "I'm the most honest person you'll ever meet."

- **Date:** September 12, 2016
- **Situation:** Remarks during a campaign event
- **Correct Response:** Claims of personal honesty are subjective. Trump faced numerous controversies and allegations of dishonesty, leading to debates about the accuracy and truthfulness of his statements.

Trumpism: "We have the best economy ever."

- **Date:** October 11, 2019

- **Situation:** Remarks on economic performance
- **Correct Response:** Economic performance can be measured in various ways, and comparisons with past periods are complex. While the economy showed growth before the pandemic, labeling it the "best ever" overlooks other historical periods of economic success.

Trumpism: "I never said I was against testing for COVID-19."

- **Date:** June 16, 2020
- **Situation:** Remarks during a press briefing
- **Correct Response:** Trump had previously made statements minimizing the importance of testing. His later remarks contradict earlier comments where he questioned or downplayed the significance of widespread testing.

Trumpism: "I'm the most successful president ever."

- **Date:** September 18, 2020
- **Situation:** Remarks during a campaign rally
- **Correct Response:** Evaluating presidential success is subjective and depends on various metrics and historical contexts. Different presidents have achieved significant successes in various areas, making comparisons complex.

Trumpism: "The fake news media is making everything worse."

- **Date:** August 5, 2020
- **Situation:** Remarks on media coverage
- **Correct Response:** Media coverage can influence public perception, but attributing all negative outcomes to "fake news" oversimplifies the range of factors affecting events and issues.

Trumpism: "We're getting rid of Obamacare, and it's going to be wonderful."

- **Date:** November 29, 2016
- **Situation:** Remarks during a transition period before his presidency
- **Correct Response:** Efforts to repeal and replace the Affordable Care Act (Obamacare) led to various legislative proposals but did not result in a comprehensive replacement. The effects of the attempts to dismantle Obamacare remain debated.

Trumpism: "The virus is going to go away with the warm weather."

- **Date:** February 10, 2020
- **Situation:** Remarks during a press briefing
- **Correct Response:** COVID-19 did not significantly diminish with warmer weather. The virus continued to spread regardless of seasonal temperature changes, highlighting the need for continued public health measures.

Trumpism: "I'm a very stable genius."

- **Date:** January 6, 2018
- **Situation:** Remarks in a tweet
- **Correct Response:** Claims of being a "stable genius" are subjective and not subject to objective validation. Evaluations of mental and intellectual stability involve comprehensive assessments beyond self-claims.

Trumpism: "We have done more for the African American community than any other administration."

- **Date:** January 4, 2020
- **Situation:** Remarks during a campaign rally

- **Correct Response:** The impact of policies on the African American community involves complex assessments and comparisons with other administrations. Various programs and issues affect different communities in diverse ways.

Trumpism: "There's no such thing as climate change."

- **Date:** June 1, 2017
- **Situation:** Remarks during the announcement of withdrawing from the Paris Agreement
- **Correct Response:** Climate change is a well-documented phenomenon supported by extensive scientific research. Denying its existence contradicts the consensus among climate scientists and evidence of global temperature changes.

Trumpism: "I'm not worried about the economy. It's going to be great."

- **Date:** March 25, 2020
- **Situation:** Remarks during a press briefing amid the COVID-19 pandemic
- **Correct Response:** The economy faced significant challenges due to the pandemic, including job losses and economic downturns. The statement underestimated the severe impact of the crisis on economic conditions.

Trumpism: "The polls are all wrong. I'm winning by a lot."

- **Date:** October 22, 2020
- **Situation:** Remarks during a campaign rally
- **Correct Response:** Polls and surveys provide data based on samples of public opinion. While polls can vary in accuracy, predictions were consistent with the actual election outcomes, which were verified by official results.

Trumpism: "The election is being rigged."

- **Date:** October 17, 2020
- **Situation:** Remarks on election integrity
- **Correct Response:** Claims of widespread election rigging were not substantiated by evidence. Multiple audits, recounts, and investigations confirmed the integrity of the election process.

Trumpism: "I have done more for the economy than any president in history."

- **Date:** February 11, 2020
- **Situation:** Remarks during a press briefing
- **Correct Response:** Economic performance and achievements are measured by various factors and comparisons. Different presidents have overseen significant economic successes and challenges, making absolute claims complex.

Trumpism: "I am the best negotiator the world has ever seen."

- **Date:** July 17, 2017
- **Situation:** Remarks during a press briefing
- **Correct Response:** The effectiveness of negotiation skills is subjective and varies by context. While Trump has been involved in various deals, assessments of his negotiation skills can differ among observers.

Trumpism: "We're not taking any responsibility for the virus."

- **Date:** March 15, 2020
- **Situation:** Remarks during a press briefing
- **Correct Response:** The federal government plays a role in managing public health crises, including COVID-19. The statement reflects a perspective that may overlook the complexities

of governmental responsibilities and responses.

Trumpism: "The U.S. economy is booming like never before."

- **Date:** January 2, 2020
- **Situation:** Remarks on economic performance
- **Correct Response:** The economy showed growth before the COVID-19 pandemic, but the claim of unprecedented booming does not account for historical economic periods with similar or greater levels of growth.

Trumpism: "I've done more for the Jewish community than any other president."

- **Date:** December 16, 2019
- **Situation:** Remarks during a campaign event
- **Correct Response:** Evaluating contributions to specific communities involves various factors and perspectives. Different administrations have had varied impacts on the Jewish community through policies and relations.

Trumpism: "The coronavirus is just a hoax."

- **Date:** February 28, 2020
- **Situation:** Remarks during a campaign rally
- **Correct Response:** COVID-19 is a real and serious global pandemic. Referring to it as a "hoax" contradicted the evidence and severity of the virus, which affected millions worldwide.

Trumpism: "I have a great relationship with the press."

- **Date:** June 15, 2019
- **Situation:** Remarks during a press briefing
- **Correct Response:** The relationship between Trump and the press

was often contentious, with frequent criticisms of media coverage. The claim of a "great" relationship contrasts with the ongoing tensions and disputes.

Trumpism: "We are the safest country in the world."

- **Date:** September 24, 2019
- **Situation:** Remarks during a UN General Assembly speech
- **Correct Response:** Safety and security vary by context and are influenced by various factors. While the U.S. has strong security measures, it faces diverse challenges and risks affecting safety.

Trumpism: "I'm a genius with numbers."

- **Date:** April 10, 2019
- **Situation:** Remarks during a financial discussion
- **Correct Response:** Claims of being a "genius" with numbers are subjective and not verified through objective measures. Expertise in financial matters involves detailed and accurate financial analysis.

Trumpism: "I never said Russia was involved in the election."

- **Date:** July 16, 2018
- **Situation:** Remarks following a summit with Vladimir Putin
- **Correct Response:** Trump had previously acknowledged Russian interference in the 2016 election. The statement contradicted past comments and findings from various investigations.

Trumpism: "I'm not interested in getting involved in foreign wars."

- **Date:** May 12, 2016
- **Situation:** Remarks during a campaign event
- **Correct Response:** The U.S. engaged in various international conflicts and military operations during Trump's presidency,

making the claim of non-involvement in foreign wars complex and subject to interpretation.

Trumpism: "I will always protect Social Security."

- **Date:** July 17, 2018
- **Situation:** Remarks on Social Security during a press briefing
- **Correct Response:** Policy proposals and budget decisions affecting Social Security varied. While Trump made statements about protecting the program, specific policy actions and budget impacts are subject to detailed evaluation.

Trumpism: "The media is lying about the crowd size."

- **Date:** January 21, 2017
- **Situation:** Remarks regarding the inauguration crowd size
- **Correct Response:** Estimates of crowd size for events can vary. Independent assessments and photographic evidence provided a more accurate depiction of the crowd size compared to the initial claims.

Trumpism: "We have the cleanest air and water in the world."

- **Date:** September 4, 2019
- **Situation:** Remarks on environmental policies
- **Correct Response:** Environmental quality varies by region and metric. While the U.S. has made improvements in some areas, it also faces challenges regarding air and water quality compared to other countries.

Trumpism: "I'm the most successful businessman ever."

- **Date:** November 3, 2016
- **Situation:** Remarks during a campaign rally

- **Correct Response:** Success in business is measured by various criteria, including financial performance and industry impact. Comparisons with other successful business figures involve complex evaluations.

Trumpism: "I never said anything about the virus being a hoax."

- **Date:** September 10, 2020
- **Situation:** Remarks during a press briefing
- **Correct Response:** Trump had previously made statements minimizing the severity of the virus, which were interpreted by some as downplaying its seriousness, leading to confusion and controversy.

Trumpism: "The U.S. economy was the strongest in history."

- **Date:** December 15, 2019
- **Situation:** Remarks on economic achievements
- **Correct Response:** Economic strength can be evaluated through various indicators. While the economy showed growth before the COVID-19 pandemic, comparisons with historical data reveal periods of significant economic performance.

Trumpism: "I've done more to lower taxes than any other president."

- **Date:** March 22, 2018
- **Situation:** Remarks on tax reform
- **Correct Response:** Tax reforms and cuts vary in scope and impact. While Trump's administration implemented significant tax changes, comparisons with other presidents involve evaluating the extent and effects of tax policies.

Trumpism: "The economy will recover quickly after the pandemic."

- **Date:** May 5, 2020
- **Situation:** Remarks on economic recovery
- **Correct Response:** The economic recovery from the pandemic faced numerous challenges and was slower than anticipated. The statement underestimated the complexities of the economic impact and recovery process.

Trumpism: "I have the highest approval rating of any president."

- **Date:** June 7, 2019
- **Situation:** Remarks during a press briefing
- **Correct Response:** Approval ratings vary over time and are subject to numerous factors. While Trump had high approval ratings at certain points, historical data shows varied ratings compared to other presidents.

Trumpism: "The economy was in the best shape ever before the pandemic."

- **Date:** October 1, 2020
- **Situation:** Remarks on economic conditions
- **Correct Response:** The economy showed strong performance before the pandemic, but labeling it as the "best shape ever" overlooks historical periods of economic prosperity and challenges.

Trumpism: "The tax cuts will pay for themselves."

- **Date:** December 6, 2017
- **Situation:** Remarks on tax reform
- **Correct Response:** The idea that tax cuts will pay for themselves is debated among economists. The long-term impact of tax cuts on revenue and economic growth involves complex analyses and projections.

Trumpism: "I know more about the environment than most people."

- **Date:** July 8, 2019
- **Situation:** Remarks during a White House meeting
- **Correct Response:** Environmental expertise generally comes from years of study and experience in environmental science, which Trump does not have. This statement is seen as an exaggeration of personal knowledge.

Trumpism: "Nobody has done more for the middle class than me."

- **Date:** September 10, 2019
- **Situation:** Remarks at a rally in North Carolina
- **Correct Response:** Economic policies impacting the middle class are complex and have varied effects. The impact of Trump's policies on the middle class is debated among economists, with mixed reviews on tax reform and healthcare changes.

Trumpism: "The U.S. has the lowest mortality rate from COVID-19."

- **Date:** July 19, 2020
- **Situation:** Remarks in a television interview
- **Correct Response:** At various points in the pandemic, the U.S. had a higher mortality rate compared to other developed countries. Data varies, but claims of having the lowest mortality were inaccurate during significant stages of the pandemic.

Trumpism: "I brought back football."

- **Date:** September 1, 2020
- **Situation:** Remarks during a press briefing
- **Correct Response:** The decision to hold college football seasons was made by various conferences and the NCAA, based on numerous factors, including state and local health guidelines,

rather than by the President alone.

Trumpism: "We built the greatest economy in the history of the world."

- **Date:** October 13, 2020
- **Situation:** Remarks during a campaign rally
- **Correct Response:** This statement is an exaggeration. While the U.S. economy was strong before the pandemic, describing it as the greatest in world history overlooks other periods of significant economic prosperity both in the U.S. and globally.

Trumpism: "We will have a vaccine very soon."

- **Date:** August 27, 2020
- **Situation:** Remarks at the Republican National Convention
- **Correct Response:** The timeline for vaccine development was optimistic. While a vaccine was indeed developed before the end of 2020, experts had cautioned that the process could take longer due to necessary testing and safety evaluations.

Trumpism: "The impeachment is a hoax."

- **Date:** December 18, 2019
- **Situation:** Remarks during the impeachment inquiry
- **Correct Response:** The impeachment process was based on evidence gathered during investigations into Trump's conduct. Calling it a "hoax" misrepresents the constitutional and legal basis on which the impeachment proceedings were founded.

Trumpism: "They're taking away your guns."

- **Date:** March 28, 2019
- **Situation:** Remarks at a rally in Michigan
- **Correct Response:** This claim often refers to proposed gun

control measures, which typically involve specific regulations like background checks or bans on certain types of firearms, rather than a blanket confiscation of all firearms from citizens.

Trumpism: "We have turned the corner on the pandemic."

- **Date:** October 20, 2020
- **Situation:** Remarks during a campaign event
- **Correct Response:** At the time of the statement, the U.S. was entering another wave of rising COVID-19 cases, contradicting the assertion that the situation was improving significantly.

Trumpism: "I am the best thing that ever happened to Puerto Rico."

- **Date:** September 16, 2020
- **Situation:** Remarks during a White House briefing
- **Correct Response:** This statement was controversial, especially in the context of criticism regarding the federal response to Hurricane Maria. Opinions in Puerto Rico about Trump's presidency were mixed, with many criticizing the level of support after the disaster.

Trumpism: "Wind energy is very expensive."

- **Date:** August 15, 2020
- **Situation:** Remarks during a campaign rally
- **Correct Response:** Wind energy has become one of the most cost-effective sources of new electricity generation, competing directly with natural gas and solar energy. The cost of wind energy has significantly decreased over the past decade due to technological advancements.

Trumpism: "We have built 500 miles of great border wall."

- **Date:** October 29, 2020

- **Situation:** Remarks at a campaign rally
- **Correct Response:** While a substantial amount of border wall was constructed, much of it replaced existing barriers rather than being new miles of wall. The exact figures and the characterization of the wall's efficacy and necessity are subjects of political debate.

Trumpism: "Our military was a disaster before I came into office."

- **Date:** September 5, 2020
- **Situation:** Remarks during a press briefing
- **Correct Response:** The U.S. military has consistently been among the most capable and well-funded in the world. While Trump increased military spending, describing it as a "disaster" before his administration is not accurate and overlooks the complex factors affecting military readiness.

Trumpism: "I will always protect people with pre-existing conditions."

- **Date:** October 22, 2020
- **Situation:** Remarks at the final presidential debate
- **Correct Response:** The administration supported lawsuits and legislative efforts that sought to overturn the Affordable Care Act, which protects individuals with pre-existing conditions. This raises questions about the consistency of the protection of these individuals under his policies.

Trumpism: "The economy is the best it's ever been, thanks to me."

- **Date:** January 30, 2020
- **Situation:** Remarks during an economic summit
- **Correct Response:** While the U.S. economy was strong prior to the COVID-19 pandemic, attributing it to a single presidency oversimplifies the broader economic trends and the efforts of various stakeholders including businesses, consumers, and previous

administrations.

Trumpism: "I've created the greatest economic recovery in history."

- **Date:** October 13, 2020
- **Situation:** Remarks during a campaign rally
- **Correct Response:** The economic recovery during and after the COVID-19 pandemic has been uneven and complex. While some sectors experienced rapid recovery, others, like hospitality and service industries, continued to struggle significantly.

Trumpism: "Mail-in voting will lead to the greatest fraud."

- **Date:** August 20, 2020
- **Situation:** Remarks during a press conference
- **Correct Response:** There is no substantial evidence to support claims that mail-in voting leads to widespread electoral fraud. Numerous studies and reports have confirmed that mail-in voting is a secure and reliable method of conducting elections.

Trumpism: "The children are brought here by coyotes and lots of bad people."

- **Date:** October 22, 2020
- **Situation:** Remarks at the final presidential debate
- **Correct Response:** While human trafficking is a serious issue, many children arrive at the border with family members or alone to escape violence and poverty, not necessarily brought by "coyotes." The situation is complex and requires a nuanced understanding of immigration dynamics.

Trumpism: "Nobody respects women more than I do."

- **Date:** October 19, 2016

- **Situation:** Remarks during the final presidential debate
- **Correct Response:** This claim has been highly contested given the numerous allegations of sexual misconduct and his recorded comments about women. Respect for women is typically demonstrated through actions and consistent behavior.

Trumpism: "Climate change is a hoax perpetrated by the Chinese."

- **Date:** November 6, 2012
- **Situation:** Tweet
- **Correct Response:** Climate change is a scientifically recognized phenomenon, affirmed by the vast majority of the scientific community worldwide. It is not a hoax and has substantial evidence documenting its impacts.

Trumpism: "I am the chosen one to fix this."

- **Date:** August 21, 2019
- **Situation:** Remarks during a press briefing
- **Correct Response:** This statement, made while discussing the trade war with China, was seen as a hyperbolic assertion of self-importance and has been widely criticized for its messianic overtones.

Trumpism: "We have the best testing system in the world."

- **Date:** May 15, 2020
- **Situation:** Remarks during a White House briefing on COVID-19
- **Correct Response:** While the U.S. ramped up its testing capabilities over time, there were significant issues with testing delays and availability in the early months of the pandemic. Many countries with more effective testing and tracing systems had better control over the virus spread.

Trumpism: "I did more for Christianity and for religion itself than anybody else."

- **Date:** December 5, 2020
- **Situation:** Remarks during a campaign event
- **Correct Response:** This statement is highly subjective. While Trump implemented policies favorable to some religious groups, such as evangelical Christians, measuring his impact against "anybody else" is not quantifiable and overlooks significant religious figures and other presidents' contributions.

Trumpism: "The coronavirus is going away."

- **Date:** October 10, 2020
- **Situation:** Remarks during a campaign rally
- **Correct Response:** At the time of these remarks, COVID-19 was not going away and was instead surging in many parts of the United States. Public health officials continued to warn about the seriousness of the pandemic and the need for preventive measures.

Trumpism: "They spied on my campaign."

- **Date:** May 17, 2018
- **Situation:** Tweet regarding the investigation into Russian interference in the 2016 election
- **Correct Response:** There is no evidence that the Obama administration ordered the FBI to spy on Trump's campaign. The FBI conducted an authorized investigation into Russian contacts with Trump's campaign, which is standard procedure in counterintelligence probes.

Trumpism: "I know windmills very much."

- **Date:** December 22, 2019

- **Situation:** Remarks during a speech on environmental policies
- **Correct Response:** Trump has made multiple incorrect claims about wind energy, including that wind turbines cause cancer and are a major source of bird deaths. Experts in renewable energy have debunked these claims, noting the benefits of wind power as a clean energy source.

Trumpism: "We're rounding the turn on the pandemic."

- **Date:** October 24, 2020
- **Situation:** Remarks at a campaign rally
- **Correct Response:** This statement was made during a time when COVID-19 cases were actually rising significantly in the United States. Public health data did not support the claim that the pandemic was nearing its end.

Trumpism: "I brought back manufacturing."

- **Date:** September 30, 2020
- **Situation:** Remarks during a presidential debate
- **Correct Response:** While some manufacturing jobs returned to the U.S. during Trump's presidency, the overall trend of manufacturing in America involves complex global economic factors. The sector continued to face challenges, including automation and overseas competition.

Trumpism: "There were millions of illegal votes."

- **Date:** November 27, 2016
- **Situation:** Tweet claiming widespread voter fraud
- **Correct Response:** There is no evidence to support claims of millions of illegal votes in the 2016 election. Multiple studies and investigations have shown that voter fraud is extremely rare in the United States.

Trumpism: "I'm the least racist person in this room."

- **Date:** October 22, 2020
- **Situation:** Response during the second presidential debate
- **Correct Response:** This claim has been widely contested given Trump's history of making racially insensitive remarks and implementing policies considered by many as discriminatory. Assessments of racism are subjective and depend on the interpretation of actions and words over time.

Trumpism: "The economy is the best it's ever been because of me."

- **Date:** January 30, 2020
- **Situation:** Remarks during an economic summit
- **Correct Response:** While the economy was indeed strong before the COVID-19 pandemic, attributing it as the "best ever" is an oversimplification. Economic health is influenced by a multitude of factors, including global economic trends and policies set by previous administrations.

Trumpism: "I've done more for peace than any president ever."

- **Date:** September 15, 2020
- **Situation:** Remarks following the signing of the Abraham Accords
- **Correct Response:** While the Abraham Accords represented a significant diplomatic achievement, the claim of doing "more for peace than any president ever" overlooks substantial peace agreements brokered under other administrations, such as the Camp David Accords and the Good Friday Agreement.

Trumpism: "Nobody knows technology like me."

- **Date:** March 6, 2018
- **Situation:** Remarks during a technology summit

- **Correct Response:** This statement is hyperbolic. While Trump has been involved in businesses that use technology, experts in fields like IT, software development, and engineering have far deeper and practical knowledge of technology.

Trumpism: "The Democrats want to destroy your suburbs."

- **Date:** July 29, 2020
- **Situation:** Remarks during a White House briefing
- **Correct Response:** This claim misrepresents housing policies proposed by Democrats, which aim to expand affordable housing options. The rhetoric about destroying suburbs is a fear-mongering tactic that lacks a factual basis.

Trumpism: "We have built a tremendous wall."

- **Date:** October 13, 2020
- **Situation:** Remarks at a campaign event
- **Correct Response:** As of late 2020, much of the border wall construction replaced existing barriers rather than adding new lengths. The total new construction did not cover the entire U.S.-Mexico border as initially promised.

Trumpism: "I am the best at the military."

- **Date:** November 12, 2019
- **Situation:** Remarks at a Veterans Day event
- **Correct Response:** This claim is an exaggeration. Effective military leadership is complex and involves decisions that are strategic and informed by military experts and long-standing defense protocols.

Trumpism: "We will have a vaccine by Election Day."

- **Date:** August 6, 2020
- **Situation:** Remarks in a television interview
- **Correct Response:** The prediction did not materialize as stated. While significant progress was made on the vaccine front, it was not approved and widely available until after the November 2020 election.

Trumpism: "The coronavirus numbers are down, and it's safe to reopen the country."

- **Date:** May 11, 2020
- **Situation:** Remarks during a press briefing
- **Correct Response:** At the time, coronavirus cases were not consistently decreasing nationwide, and many health experts warned about the risks of reopening too early without adequate safety measures in place.

Trumpism: "Antifa is the real problem."

- **Date:** June 1, 2020
- **Situation:** Remarks during a law enforcement briefing
- **Correct Response:** This statement attempts to attribute widespread civil unrest and violence to a single group, which oversimplifies the complex dynamics of protests that were largely driven by issues of racial injustice and police brutality. Antifa, a loosely connected movement of anti-fascist groups, was not the primary source of violence.

Trumpism: "I saved pre-existing conditions."

- **Date:** January 13, 2020
- **Situation:** Tweet
- **Correct Response:** The Affordable Care Act, which Trump and his administration repeatedly attempted to repeal and weaken,

originally protected people with pre-existing conditions. Claims of saving these protections contradict efforts by his administration that would have undermined them.

Trumpism: "I've made the military strong again."

- **Date:** October 26, 2020
- **Situation:** Remarks at a campaign rally
- **Correct Response:** While defense spending increased under Trump's administration, the U.S. military has consistently been among the most powerful globally. The assertion that it was not strong before his tenure oversimplifies the continuous investments and advancements made across multiple administrations.

Trumpism: "I will totally protect Social Security."

- **Date:** February 13, 2020
- **Situation:** Tweet
- **Correct Response:** Despite this claim, budget proposals from Trump's administration included cuts to Social Security disability insurance. Protecting Social Security in its entirety would require maintaining or increasing funding without reductions.

Trumpism: "I've been the best president for Black Americans, with the possible exception of Lincoln."

- **Date:** August 11, 2020
- **Situation:** Remarks in an interview
- **Correct Response:** This statement overlooks significant civil rights advancements made by other presidents, such as Lyndon B. Johnson, who signed the Civil Rights Act and Voting Rights Act. The impact of any presidency on a specific community can vary and is deeply complex.

Trumpism: "The election is rigged if I don't win."

- **Date:** October 27, 2020
- **Situation:** Remarks at a campaign rally
- **Correct Response:** The integrity of the U.S. electoral process has been upheld by numerous studies and state officials, including those from Trump's own administration. Declaring an election rigged without evidence undermines the democratic process.

Trumpism: "We're the envy of the world right now."

- **Date:** July 5, 2020
- **Situation:** Remarks during a White House event
- **Correct Response:** This statement was made during the global COVID-19 pandemic when the U.S. was experiencing one of the highest rates of infection and death. Many countries were managing the pandemic more effectively, which contradicts the notion of universal envy.

Trumpism: "Nobody does the environment like we do."

- **Date:** October 14, 2020
- **Situation:** Remarks during a town hall
- **Correct Response:** The U.S. has faced criticism, especially from environmentalists and international leaders, for rolling back numerous environmental protections during Trump's presidency. This claim overlooks those actions and their impacts on national and global environmental standards.

Trumpism: "I know more about drones than anybody."

- **Date:** July 31, 2020
- **Situation:** Remarks during a technology briefing
- **Correct Response:** This is an unlikely claim, given the specialized

knowledge required in fields like aerospace engineering, military strategy, and surveillance technologies, which experts in those fields would possess.

Trumpism: "We're doing more testing than anybody in the world."

- **Date:** May 20, 2020
- **Situation:** Remarks during a press conference
- **Correct Response:** At various times, the U.S. led in the raw number of tests conducted, but when adjusted for population, several other countries had higher testing rates. Moreover, effective testing also includes timeliness and the ability to process and act on the results efficiently.

Trumpism: "No president has ever done what I have done for seniors."

- **Date:** October 16, 2020
- **Situation:** Remarks during a rally in Florida
- **Correct Response:** This statement overlooks significant legislative actions taken by previous presidents that have directly benefited senior citizens, such as the creation of Medicare and Social Security enhancements. The impact of presidential actions on seniors varies and requires a nuanced comparison.

Trumpism: "I saved millions of jobs during the pandemic."

- **Date:** June 5, 2020
- **Situation:** Remarks at a press briefing on employment rates
- **Correct Response:** While government interventions, including those signed into law by Trump, helped mitigate job losses during the pandemic, the claim of saving millions of jobs doesn't account for the complex economic factors involved and the temporary nature of some job recoveries.

Trumpism: "I am the least racist person there is anywhere in the world."

- **Date:** July 30, 2019
- **Situation:** Remarks to reporters at the White House
- **Correct Response:** Claims about personal levels of racism are inherently subjective. Trump's statement is controversial and has been widely debated, especially considering his administration's policies and various remarks seen by many as racially insensitive.

Trumpism: "We have the most advanced healthcare system in the world."

- **Date:** March 27, 2020
- **Situation:** Remarks during a White House Coronavirus Task Force briefing
- **Correct Response:** While the U.S. healthcare system is advanced in terms of technology and resources, its accessibility and cost issues, along with the health outcomes it produces, often do not compare favorably with those of other developed nations.

Trumpism: "The Democrats are trying to rig this election because it's the only way they're going to win."

- **Date:** September 2, 2020
- **Situation:** Remarks during a press briefing
- **Correct Response:** Accusations of election rigging need to be backed by concrete evidence. Multiple reviews and court cases found no substantial evidence of widespread voter fraud or rigging in the 2020 election.

Trumpism: "Wind turbines are a bird graveyard."

- **Date:** August 13, 2020
- **Situation:** Remarks during a campaign event

- **Correct Response:** While wind turbines do cause some bird deaths, the impact is significantly less than that caused by other human activities such as building windows or cats. The renewable energy sector is actively working on solutions to further minimize these impacts.

Trumpism: "Under my administration, we have achieved energy dominance."

- **Date:** July 8, 2020
- **Situation:** Remarks at an energy sector meeting
- **Correct Response:** The U.S. has become a leading producer of oil and natural gas, largely due to technological advances in hydraulic fracturing and horizontal drilling. However, the concept of "energy dominance" oversimplifies global energy dependencies and market dynamics.

Trumpism: "I have the best environmental record of any president."

- **Date:** October 14, 2020
- **Situation:** Remarks during a town hall meeting
- **Correct Response:** Trump's administration rolled back numerous environmental regulations, which many experts argue has harmed environmental protection efforts. Evaluating his record against those of presidents who expanded regulatory protections shows a stark contrast.

Trumpism: "Our numbers are the best in terms of coronavirus."

- **Date:** July 21, 2020
- **Situation:** Remarks during a press briefing
- **Correct Response:** At the time of these remarks, the U.S. was leading the world in both confirmed COVID-19 cases and deaths, which contrasts with the implication of having "the best" numbers.

Trumpism: "We are the greatest country in the history of the world."

- **Date:** July 4, 2020
- **Situation:** Remarks during Independence Day celebrations
- **Correct Response:** This statement reflects national pride but is subjective and cannot be quantitatively measured. Different countries excel in various aspects such as economic strength, quality of life, innovation, and cultural influence.

Trumpism: "I think solar energy is very expensive."

- **Date:** June 25, 2020
- **Situation:** Remarks during an energy policy discussion
- **Correct Response:** The cost of solar energy has dramatically decreased over the past decade, making it one of the cheapest sources of new electricity generation in many parts of the world, including the United States.

Trumpism: "Nobody's done more for the military than I have."

- **Date:** September 7, 2020
- **Situation:** Remarks during a Labor Day press conference
- **Correct Response:** While the Trump administration has increased military spending, measuring contributions to the military is complex and includes considerations of veterans' care, strategic decisions, and overall military effectiveness across different presidencies.

Trumpism: "We're rounding the final turn on the virus."

- **Date:** September 10, 2020
- **Situation:** Remarks during a campaign rally
- **Correct Response:** At the time of this statement, new cases of COVID-19 were increasing in several U.S. regions, indicating that

the pandemic was far from over. Public health officials continued to urge caution and preventive measures.

Trumpism: "I am the builder president."

- **Date:** August 4, 2020
- **Situation:** Remarks at a White House event
- **Correct Response:** Trump often highlighted his background in real estate development as evidence of his capability to manage infrastructure projects. However, significant new infrastructure legislation was not passed during his presidency.

Trumpism: "The children are being brought over by smugglers and traffickers."

- **Date:** October 22, 2020
- **Situation:** Remarks during the second presidential debate
- **Correct Response:** While some children are brought to the U.S. border by smugglers, many come with family members or alone to escape violence and poverty in their home countries. The situation is complex, requiring a nuanced understanding of migration.

Trumpism: "Our numbers are better than almost all countries."

- **Date:** August 5, 2020
- **Situation:** Remarks on COVID-19 statistics
- **Correct Response:** The U.S. had one of the highest numbers of confirmed COVID-19 cases and deaths at this time, indicating significant challenges in managing the pandemic compared to other countries with lower rates per capita.

Trumpism: "They say I have the most loyal people — did you ever see that?"

- **Date:** January 16, 2020
- **Situation:** Remarks during a campaign event
- **Correct Response:** Trump's base has shown high levels of loyalty in polls and elections. However, measuring "the most loyal people" is subjective and can vary depending on the metrics used.

Trumpism: "I will have the best Cabinet that anybody has ever had."

- **Date:** December 15, 2016
- **Situation:** Remarks after the election
- **Correct Response:** The effectiveness and quality of a presidential cabinet can be subjective and varies based on individual performance, expertise, and the administration's overall success. Several of Trump's Cabinet members faced controversy or resigned under pressure.

Trumpism: "We have the best testing in the world. That's why we have more cases."

- **Date:** May 19, 2020
- **Situation:** Remarks during a cabinet meeting
- **Correct Response:** While the U.S. ramped up testing, the high number of COVID-19 cases was not solely due to more testing but also widespread community transmission. Experts noted that testing alone cannot account for the higher rates of infection and emphasized the importance of other factors like virus spread.

Trumpism: "We won the election by a landslide."

- **Date:** December 2, 2020
- **Situation:** Remarks during a White House event
- **Correct Response:** The 2020 presidential election results showed Joe Biden winning both the popular vote and the Electoral College. There was no evidence of the widespread voter fraud

claimed by Trump, and his assertion of a landslide victory is factually incorrect.

Trumpism: "I've been tougher on Russia than any other president."

- **Date:** July 18, 2018
- **Situation:** Remarks during a press conference
- **Correct Response:** While his administration did implement several rounds of sanctions against Russia, historical actions by other presidents, like Reagan's diplomatic pressures during the Cold War, also show significant toughness. This statement simplifies a complex historical context.

Trumpism: "Our farmers are doing better than ever before."

- **Date:** January 15, 2020
- **Situation:** Remarks at the signing of the Phase One trade deal with China
- **Correct Response:** The U.S. farming sector faced significant challenges during Trump's presidency, including trade wars that harmed exports and lowered prices for farm goods. While some aid was provided, the claim that farmers were doing better than ever does not capture the full economic impact on the sector.

Trumpism: "The media is the real virus."

- **Date:** March 22, 2020
- **Situation:** Tweet
- **Correct Response:** This statement metaphorically criticizes the media, implying that their coverage is harmful. It's an expression of discontent with how the media reported on his administration's handling of the COVID-19 pandemic, but it inaccurately conflates journalistic reporting with the spread of a biological virus.

Trumpism: "We have built the strongest economy in the history of the world."

- **Date:** February 4, 2020
- **Situation:** Remarks during the State of the Union address
- **Correct Response:** The U.S. economy was performing well prior to the COVID-19 pandemic with low unemployment and growth, but stating it was the strongest in the history of the world is hyperbolic and ignores periods of similar or greater growth in the U.S. and other nations.

Trumpism: "Everything we've done is 100% proper."

- **Date:** January 10, 2018
- **Situation:** Remarks to reporters
- **Correct Response:** This assertion came in response to investigations into potential collusion and obstruction of justice. Various actions and decisions of his administration were legally contested and led to numerous investigations, indicating complex legal and ethical challenges.

Trumpism: "We're the best in the world at fighting the coronavirus."

- **Date:** May 11, 2020
- **Situation:** Remarks during a press briefing
- **Correct Response:** At that time, the U.S. was leading the world in both confirmed cases and deaths from COVID-19, challenging the claim about being the best at combating the virus. Other countries were noted for their more effective responses and lower case rates.

Trumpism: "I am the best at the military. No one has ever seen anything like what I've done."

- **Date:** August 28, 2020

- **Situation:** Remarks to military personnel
- **Correct Response:** This hyperbolic statement overlooks the continuous and complex contributions of past presidents who have engaged in major conflicts and overseen significant military operations and innovations.

Trumpism: "I did what no other president has ever done."

- **Date:** June 4, 2020
- **Situation:** Remarks during a press briefing about economic gains
- **Correct Response:** While Trump did implement unique policies and approaches during his presidency, the claim to have done things no other president has ever done is an exaggeration. Many of his actions were unprecedented in style rather than substance, and all presidents have their unique achievements.

Trumpism: "I know more about NATO than most people."

- **Date:** October 17, 2020
- **Situation:** Remarks during a town hall
- **Correct Response:** This statement overstates personal expertise. NATO is a complex military and political alliance that requires detailed knowledge of history, military strategy, and international relations, typically studied by experts in those fields.

Trumpism: "Nobody respects the office more than I do."

- **Date:** July 29, 2019
- **Situation:** Remarks during a Cabinet meeting
- **Correct Response:** Respect for the office of the presidency is demonstrated through actions and adherence to norms and protocols. Critics have argued that some of Trump's actions and words were not in keeping with traditional respect for the office.

Trumpism: "We're doing a great job with COVID-19."

- **Date:** August 3, 2020
- **Situation:** Remarks during a press briefing
- **Correct Response:** The U.S. faced significant challenges in handling the COVID-19 pandemic, including testing shortages and high infection rates compared to other developed countries. The response was widely criticized by public health officials for being fragmented and inconsistent.

Trumpism: "The border wall has stopped the virus."

- **Date:** July 28, 2020
- **Situation:** Remarks during a briefing on border security
- **Correct Response:** The statement that the border wall has stopped the virus is misleading. COVID-19 spread within the U.S. primarily through community transmission, and public health measures such as social distancing, mask-wearing, and vaccination are the primary tools for controlling its spread.

Trumpism: "I have rebuilt the military."

- **Date:** November 5, 2020
- **Situation:** Remarks during a campaign rally
- **Correct Response:** Trump increased military spending and funded several large-scale defense projects. However, the U.S. military has been continually funded and modernized by successive administrations, and it remained robust before his presidency.

Trumpism: "We have achieved American energy independence."

- **Date:** September 8, 2020
- **Situation:** Remarks at a campaign event
- **Correct Response:** While the U.S. has become a net exporter of

oil and natural gas, it still imports substantial amounts of crude oil. True energy independence would involve a complete disengagement from global oil markets, which has not been achieved.

Trumpism: "Our testing has put us at the top of the world."

- **Date:** July 21, 2020
- **Situation:** Remarks during a press briefing
- **Correct Response:** While the U.S. conducted a high number of COVID-19 tests, the testing rate per capita was not the highest in the world. Issues with testing delays and access were significant, especially in the early months of the pandemic.

Trumpism: "I have the best financial instincts."

- **Date:** August 12, 2020
- **Situation:** Remarks during a business roundtable
- **Correct Response:** Financial acumen is subjective and difficult to measure definitively. While Trump has had successes in real estate, his businesses have also faced bankruptcies and financial struggles, suggesting a more mixed record.

Trumpism: "I've done more for the environment than any other president."

- **Date:** July 29, 2020
- **Situation:** Remarks during an environmental policy announcement
- **Correct Response:** This claim is contested by environmentalists and experts who point out that his administration rolled back numerous environmental protections, including regulations on air and water pollution and withdrawing from the Paris Climate Agreement.

Trumpism: "We have signed more legislation than any other president."

- **Date:** December 22, 2017
- **Situation:** Remarks before signing tax legislation
- **Correct Response:** By the end of his first year in office, Trump had signed fewer pieces of legislation than any first-year president since Eisenhower. The statement is inaccurate when compared to the legislative records of other presidents at similar points in their terms.

Trumpism: "I will always protect your Second Amendment."

- **Date:** September 20, 2019
- **Situation:** Remarks during a campaign rally
- **Correct Response:** Trump consistently opposed significant gun control measures, aligning with a strong pro-Second Amendment stance. However, his administration did enact a ban on bump stocks following the Las Vegas shooting in 2017.

Trumpism: "We are winning the war against the virus."

- **Date:** April 15, 2020
- **Situation:** Remarks during a White House briefing
- **Correct Response:** At the time of this statement, the U.S. was struggling with a significant surge in COVID-19 cases, and many states were far from controlling the spread of the virus, contradicting the claim of "winning."

Trumpism: "No president has ever been tougher on China than me."

- **Date:** May 14, 2019
- **Situation:** Remarks during trade negotiations
- **Correct Response:** While Trump implemented aggressive trade policies against China, including tariffs and sanctions, the

effectiveness and toughness can be debated, especially considering the broader historical context of U.S.-China relations.

Trumpism: "We built the most beautiful economy in the world."

- **Date:** October 8, 2020
- **Situation:** Remarks during a presidential debate
- **Correct Response:** This hyperbolic statement simplifies complex economic issues. While the U.S. economy was performing well prior to the pandemic, describing it as "the most beautiful" overlooks ongoing issues such as income inequality and healthcare affordability.

Trumpism: "Our country is in the best shape ever."

- **Date:** February 4, 2020
- **Situation:** Remarks during the State of the Union Address
- **Correct Response:** This broad statement is highly subjective. While some economic indicators were positive, other areas like national unity and political polarization suggested significant challenges.

Trumpism: "I know more about warfare than any modern president."

- **Date:** August 11, 2020
- **Situation:** Remarks at a press conference
- **Correct Response:** This claim is difficult to substantiate. Military strategy and history are complex fields typically studied by career military professionals and historians. Past presidents, particularly those with military backgrounds, would likely be better versed in such matters.

Trumpism: "We've done a fantastic job with COVID-19."

- **Date:** September 10, 2020
- **Situation:** Remarks during a White House event
- **Correct Response:** The U.S. faced significant criticism for its handling of the COVID-19 pandemic, including issues with testing, supplies, and a coordinated response. Many public health experts disagreed with the assessment of a "fantastic job."

Trumpism: "I've achieved more than any other president in history."

- **Date:** June 16, 2020
- **Situation:** Remarks during a campaign rally
- **Correct Response:** While President Trump did achieve significant policy milestones, such as tax reform and judicial appointments, the claim to have achieved more than any other president is subjective and not supported by historical evidence when considering the full spectrum of presidential achievements.

Trumpism: "We have the cleanest air and water ever."

- **Date:** April 22, 2020
- **Situation:** Remarks on Earth Day
- **Correct Response:** While the U.S. has made strides in improving air and water quality over the decades, these statements are misleading. Environmental rollbacks during Trump's administration have raised concerns among scientists and environmentalists about the potential negative impacts on air and water quality.

Trumpism: "I'm the most pro-life president in history."

- **Date:** January 24, 2020
- **Situation:** Remarks at the March for Life rally
- **Correct Response:** President Trump did implement policies that were highly favorable to the pro-life agenda, such as appointing

conservative judges and restricting federal funding for abortions. However, the extent to which he is the "most" pro-life depends on the criteria used for comparison with other presidents.

Trumpism: "We're the best at cyber."

- **Date:** August 27, 2020
- **Situation:** Remarks during a cybersecurity briefing
- **Correct Response:** The U.S. is a leader in many areas of cybersecurity, but the statement overlooks ongoing challenges, such as vulnerabilities in critical infrastructure and significant cyber attacks from foreign adversaries.

Trumpism: "I've saved millions of lives during this pandemic."

- **Date:** September 9, 2020
- **Situation:** Remarks during a press briefing
- **Correct Response:** This claim is difficult to verify. While actions taken by the federal government have had impacts, the U.S. also experienced one of the highest COVID-19 death rates per capita among developed nations. The effectiveness of the pandemic response is widely debated.

Trumpism: "I will bring our jobs back."

- **Date:** May 14, 2020
- **Situation:** Remarks during a factory visit
- **Correct Response:** While some manufacturing jobs returned to the U.S., the overall trend of globalization continues to challenge domestic job creation in certain industries. Economic policies can influence job markets, but they cannot entirely reverse global economic trends.

Trumpism: "We have ended the war on American Energy."

- **Date:** January 30, 2018
- **Situation:** Remarks during the State of the Union address
- **Correct Response:** Trump's policies significantly favored fossil fuel industries, but characterizing previous regulatory policies as a "war" is misleading. Energy policy debates focus on balancing economic, environmental, and health considerations.

Trumpism: "I fixed the Veterans Administration."

- **Date:** November 11, 2018
- **Situation:** Remarks on Veterans Day
- **Correct Response:** While there were reforms and improvements in the Veterans Administration under Trump, such as the VA MISSION Act, challenges persist, including issues with healthcare quality and access. The claim of "fixing" simplifies the ongoing nature of these challenges.

Trumpism: "I know more about infrastructure than any other president."

- **Date:** July 29, 2019
- **Situation:** Remarks during an infrastructure meeting
- **Correct Response:** Trump's background in real estate development may have provided him with insights into certain aspects of infrastructure, but expertise in national infrastructure policy is a complex field that encompasses much more than construction, including public policy, economics, and engineering.

Trumpism: "We have the best economy in history thanks to my policies."

- **Date:** October 30, 2020
- **Situation:** Remarks during a campaign event
- **Correct Response:** While the economy experienced growth under

Trump's administration, particularly pre-COVID-19, attributing it as the "best economy in history" is an oversimplification. Economic growth was continuing a trend from previous years, and comparisons across different historical periods can be misleading without considering various economic indicators.

Trumpism: "No one has done more for Black Americans than I have, maybe with the exception of Abraham Lincoln."

- **Date:** June 16, 2020
- **Situation:** Interview with a news channel
- **Correct Response:** This statement overlooks significant legislative and civil rights achievements by other presidents such as Lyndon B. Johnson, who signed the Civil Rights Act and Voting Rights Act. While Trump did enact policies benefiting some minority communities, his claim is seen as an exaggeration.

Trumpism: "The coronavirus will disappear like a miracle."

- **Date:** February 27, 2020
- **Situation:** Remarks during a White House meeting
- **Correct Response:** This statement was overly optimistic and scientifically unfounded. The COVID-19 virus required significant global public health efforts to manage, including social distancing, vaccinations, and extensive medical research.

Trumpism: "Windmills are one of the worst sources of energy."

- **Date:** December 21, 2019
- **Situation:** Remarks during a campaign rally
- **Correct Response:** Wind energy is one of the fastest-growing and cleanest sources of renewable energy. Trump's negative comments about wind energy, including its environmental impact and efficiency, contradict the majority of scientific and environmental

research.

Trumpism: "Nobody knows more about taxes than I do, maybe in the history of the world."

- **Date:** May 12, 2016
- **Situation:** Remarks during a campaign interview
- **Correct Response:** Knowledge about taxes is typically held by tax professionals, economists, and scholars who specialize in tax law and policy. This hyperbolic claim exaggerates personal expertise in a complex field.

Trumpism: "We're going to win so much, you're going to be so sick and tired of winning."

- **Date:** May 20, 2016
- **Situation:** Remarks during a campaign rally
- **Correct Response:** This catchphrase from Trump's campaign speeches was intended to energize supporters but is subjective and not quantifiable. The notion of "winning" in policy and governance is complex and viewed differently across political and social spectrums.

Trumpism: "I'm the least racist person you will ever interview."

- **Date:** October 8, 2017
- **Situation:** Remarks during a media interview
- **Correct Response:** Claims about personal levels of racism are inherently subjective and have been widely contested in Trump's case, especially given his history of controversial remarks and policies perceived as racially insensitive.

Trumpism: "We have the most secure border in our history."

- **Date:** January 8, 2021
- **Situation:** Remarks during a visit to the border wall
- **Correct Response:** Border security involves multiple factors including personnel, technology, and physical barriers. While improvements have been made, the statement simplifies the ongoing and dynamic challenges of border security.

Trumpism: "I've saved the coal industry."

- **Date:** August 8, 2018
- **Situation:** Remarks during a rally in West Virginia
- **Correct Response:** While Trump's administration rolled back environmental regulations with the intent to revive the coal industry, the industry continued to decline due to market forces, including cheaper alternatives like natural gas and renewable energy. The claim of saving the industry does not align with ongoing economic trends and energy sector shifts.

Trumpism: "We've built the most beautiful economy in history."

- **Date:** October 24, 2020
- **Situation:** Remarks at a campaign rally in North Carolina
- **Correct Response:** While the U.S. economy was strong prior to the COVID-19 pandemic, with low unemployment and sustained growth, describing it as "the most beautiful" is subjective. Economic health is complex, influenced by various domestic and international factors over time.

Trumpism: "The wall is nearly finished."

- **Date:** September 10, 2020
- **Situation:** Remarks during a press conference
- **Correct Response:** At the time, significant portions of the border wall had been constructed or replaced, but much of the wall

promised during the 2016 campaign remained incomplete. The progress reported often involved replacement of existing barriers rather than new construction.

Trumpism: "There has never been a president who's done more than I have."

- **Date:** June 16, 2020
- **Situation:** Remarks in a television interview
- **Correct Response:** Measuring the accomplishments of a presidency is subjective and dependent on various metrics, including legislative, economic, foreign policy, and social impact. Every presidency has unique achievements and challenges, making such a comparison difficult to substantiate.

Trumpism: "We're the envy of the world."

- **Date:** July 4, 2020
- **Situation:** Remarks during Independence Day celebrations
- **Correct Response:** This statement is highly subjective. While the U.S. excels in many areas, such as technology innovation and military capability, it faces significant challenges, including healthcare, social inequality, and political division, which complicate the notion of universal envy.

Trumpism: "We have done a great job on COVID-19."

- **Date:** May 20, 2020
- **Situation:** Remarks during a factory visit
- **Correct Response:** The U.S. government's response to COVID-19 was met with significant criticism for issues such as testing delays, mixed messaging on public health guidelines, and the overall handling of the crisis compared to other developed countries.

Trumpism: "I have the best advisors."

- **Date:** April 18, 2017
- **Situation:** Remarks during a White House briefing
- **Correct Response:** The effectiveness and qualifications of advisors are subject to individual performance and the outcomes of their advice. Trump's administration experienced high turnover and numerous controversies involving his advisors, challenging this assertion.

Trumpism: "I created the greatest economy in the history of our country."

- **Date:** August 17, 2020
- **Situation:** Remarks during a campaign event
- **Correct Response:** While the economy saw significant growth and low unemployment rates before the pandemic, the claim of creating the "greatest economy" overlooks historical periods of even stronger relative growth and other economic indicators. Economic success is influenced by long-term trends often established before any single administration.

Trumpism: "We have the best COVID-19 numbers."

- **Date:** July 28, 2020
- **Situation:** Remarks during a press briefing
- **Correct Response:** At the time of this statement, the United States had one of the highest rates of COVID-19 infections and deaths globally. This claim contradicts data from the World Health Organization and the Centers for Disease Control and Prevention, which showed the U.S. struggling with managing the pandemic compared to other developed nations.

Trumpism: "I have done more for healthcare than any president."

- **Date:** September 15, 2020
- **Situation:** Remarks during a healthcare policy announcement
- **Correct Response:** Trump's administration made efforts to dismantle the Affordable Care Act and introduced some healthcare policies, such as price transparency and limited drug price controls. However, the assertion that he has done more than any president is disputed, particularly in light of expansions in healthcare access under other administrations, such as Lyndon B. Johnson and Barack Obama.

Trumpism: "I know more about foreign policy than anyone else."

- **Date:** October 9, 2019
- **Situation:** Remarks during a press conference
- **Correct Response:** Foreign policy is a complex field requiring detailed understanding of global issues, history, and diplomatic relations. This statement is an exaggeration, as expertise in foreign policy typically involves years of dedicated study and experience within international contexts.

Trumpism: "We built the greatest political movement in the history of our country."

- **Date:** February 6, 2020
- **Situation:** Remarks during a White House event
- **Correct Response:** While Trump's political movement was significant and influential, especially in terms of its impact on the Republican Party and American politics, whether it is the "greatest" is subjective and depends on how one defines "greatness." Comparisons to other historical movements like the civil rights movement or the New Deal coalition would challenge this claim.

Trumpism: "We have the lowest crime rate in our country's history."

- **Date:** June 20, 2020
- **Situation:** Remarks during a rally in Tulsa
- **Correct Response:** Crime rates in the United States have fluctuated, with significant declines from the highs of the early 1990s. While certain types of crime, like violent crime, have decreased over decades, to claim the lowest rate in history overlooks complex, localized patterns of crime across the nation.

Trumpism: "I'm the most successful businessman to become President."

- **Date:** May 4, 2017
- **Situation:** Remarks during an interview
- **Correct Response:** While Trump was a prominent businessman before his presidency, other presidents such as George Washington, Thomas Jefferson, and Theodore Roosevelt were also highly successful in their private endeavors, making this a contestable claim.

Trumpism: "Nobody has done what I've done for the suburbs."

- **Date:** September 10, 2020
- **Situation:** Remarks at a White House event
- **Correct Response:** Trump's policies aimed at preserving suburban zoning laws were seen by some as protective but by others as exacerbating racial segregation and resisting diversity. The impact and reception of these policies are mixed, depending on one's perspective on suburban development and inclusion.

Trumpism: "We've saved millions of lives."

- **Date:** October 22, 2020
- **Situation:** Remarks during a presidential debate
- **Correct Response:** This claim refers to the actions taken by Trump's administration during the COVID-19 pandemic. While

certain measures, like travel restrictions, may have mitigated the spread to some extent, the U.S. had one of the highest COVID-19 death tolls in the world at that time. Public health experts noted that a more coordinated and timely response could have significantly reduced the number of deaths.

Trumpism: "We have the strongest military we've ever had."

- **Date:** May 30, 2020
- **Situation:** Remarks at a military graduation ceremony
- **Correct Response:** The U.S. military is continually modernized and maintained as one of the world's strongest. While Trump's administration increased military spending, the claim that it is the strongest ever doesn't acknowledge the ongoing nature of military enhancements that span multiple administrations.

Trumpism: "I have been treated worse than any president in history."

- **Date:** July 9, 2020
- **Situation:** Interview with a news outlet
- **Correct Response:** This subjective claim reflects Trump's feelings about media coverage and opposition criticism. Historically, other presidents have faced severe treatments as well, including assassination and impeachment. The perception of treatment varies widely depending on political views and historical context.

Trumpism: "We built the best economy ever."

- **Date:** August 17, 2020
- **Situation:** Remarks at a campaign rally
- **Correct Response:** Prior to the pandemic, the U.S. economy was continuing a trend of growth from previous years. While unemployment was low, and the stock market was high, economists note that using "best ever" is subjective and depends on

which metrics are emphasized.

Trumpism: "I am the environmental president."

- **Date:** September 8, 2020
- **Situation:** Remarks during a campaign event
- **Correct Response:** Trump's administration rolled back numerous environmental regulations and withdrew the U.S. from the Paris Climate Agreement, actions that many environmentalists criticized as harmful to global and domestic environmental protection efforts. This claim contradicts the administration's regulatory actions.

Trumpism: "Nobody's ever done for the Hispanic community what I've done."

- **Date:** October 28, 2020
- **Situation:** Remarks at a campaign event
- **Correct Response:** While Trump enacted policies that impacted the Hispanic community, such as opportunity zones and criminal justice reform, broader claims of unparalleled benefit overlook significant legislative and executive contributions by previous presidents that directly benefited various minority communities.

Trumpism: "We have the best testing program in the world."

- **Date:** June 15, 2020
- **Situation:** Remarks during a roundtable discussion
- **Correct Response:** The U.S. ramped up its testing capabilities over time, but faced significant challenges and criticisms regarding the availability and speed of COVID-19 testing. Many countries were recognized for more effective testing strategies.

Trumpism: "The stock market is at an all-time high because of me."

- **Date:** December 14, 2019
- **Situation:** Remarks at a White House event
- **Correct Response:** While the stock market reached record levels during Trump's administration, attributing these highs solely to presidential actions oversimplifies the complex factors that influence financial markets, including global economic trends, corporate earnings, and investor sentiment.

Trumpism: "We're taking care of our veterans like never before."

- **Date:** November 11, 2019
- **Situation:** Remarks on Veterans Day
- **Correct Response:** The Trump administration implemented several policies aimed at improving veterans' care, including the VA MISSION Act. However, challenges persist in the VA system, and improvements are part of ongoing efforts that span multiple administrations.

Trumpism: "We passed the biggest tax cut in the history of our country."

- **Date:** January 30, 2020
- **Situation:** Remarks during a campaign rally
- **Correct Response:** The Tax Cuts and Jobs Act of 2017, signed by Trump, was significant but not the largest in U.S. history. It ranks behind several others, including Ronald Reagan's 1981 tax cuts and the Revenue Act of 1964 in terms of percentage of GDP and total reduction in tax liabilities.

Trumpism: "I rebuilt the U.S. military."

- **Date:** November 5, 2020
- **Situation:** Remarks at a campaign event
- **Correct Response:** Trump's administration did increase defense spending, but the U.S. military has been continuously funded and

updated, remaining the world's most powerful military force long before his presidency. The notion that it needed to be "rebuilt" oversimplifies and overlooks ongoing processes and improvements.

Trumpism: "There's never been a president as tough on Russia as I have been."

- **Date:** July 18, 2018
- **Situation:** Remarks during a press conference
- **Correct Response:** While Trump's administration did impose sanctions and other measures against Russia, critics argue that his public rhetoric often appeared conciliatory towards Vladimir Putin. Historical actions taken by other presidents, such as the economic sanctions and diplomatic measures during the Cold War, also exemplify tough stances on Russia.

Trumpism: "We have the lowest unemployment ever."

- **Date:** February 4, 2020
- **Situation:** Remarks during the State of the Union address
- **Correct Response:** Before the pandemic, the U.S. unemployment rate was at a 50-year low, but not the lowest ever. Historical data shows lower unemployment rates in the 1950s and late 1960s.

Trumpism: "I've done more for the Black community than any president since Abraham Lincoln."

- **Date:** June 2, 2020
- **Situation:** Interview with a news outlet
- **Correct Response:** While Trump signed criminal justice reform legislation and supported funding for historically Black colleges and universities, this statement overlooks significant legislative achievements by other presidents such as Lyndon B. Johnson, who signed the Civil Rights Act of 1964 and the Voting Rights Act of

1965.

Trumpism: "Our air and water are the cleanest they've ever been."

- **Date:** September 4, 2019
- **Situation:** Remarks during an environmental policy announcement
- **Correct Response:** While there have been improvements in certain areas, this claim ignores issues like declining air quality standards and regulatory rollbacks that have raised concerns among environmental scientists and advocates about potential long-term impacts on public health and natural ecosystems.

Trumpism: "We built the greatest economy in the world, very quickly."

- **Date:** October 22, 2020
- **Situation:** Remarks during a presidential debate
- **Correct Response:** The U.S. economy was already in its longest expansion period before Trump took office, which continued during his administration until the COVID-19 pandemic. The structure of this growth was influenced by both his policies and those of previous administrations.

Trumpism: "We're leading the world in environmental cleanliness."

- **Date:** July 8, 2019
- **Situation:** Remarks during an environmental meeting
- **Correct Response:** The U.S. has made strides in certain environmental metrics, but leading the world in environmental cleanliness is a broad claim that doesn't hold up under specific metrics such as carbon emissions per capita, where the U.S. ranks poorly compared to other developed nations.

Trumpism: "I'm the most transparent president, probably in the history of this country."

- **Date:** May 11, 2019
- **Situation:** Remarks during a press conference
- **Correct Response:** Trump's refusal to release his tax returns and the administration's general handling of information requests and press access have been criticized as less transparent than previous administrations. This claim contradicts observed practices regarding government transparency and media interactions.

Trumpism: "We will win so much you may even get tired of winning."

- **Date:** May 20, 2016
- **Situation:** Remarks at a campaign rally
- **Correct Response:** This catchphrase from Trump's campaign intended to convey relentless success under his leadership, but its actualization is subjective and varies widely depending on political perspectives and interpretations of policy outcomes.

Trumpism: "I've been the best president for jobs in U.S. history."

- **Date:** August 5, 2020
- **Situation:** Remarks during a White House briefing
- **Correct Response:** While the U.S. saw low unemployment rates prior to the COVID-19 pandemic under Trump's administration, the assertion of being the best president for jobs overlooks historical contexts where job growth was similarly robust. The pandemic's economic impact also significantly affected the job market during his tenure.

Trumpism: "We have the best economy in history thanks to my administration."

- **Date:** October 13, 2020
- **Situation:** Remarks during a campaign rally
- **Correct Response:** Economic success can be measured in various ways, including GDP growth, employment rates, and stock market performance. While the economy performed well pre-pandemic, claiming it as the best in history is an exaggeration and does not account for the economic downturn caused by the COVID-19 crisis.

Trumpism: "Nobody has ever built walls like I have."

- **Date:** March 10, 2018
- **Situation:** Remarks on the construction of the border wall
- **Correct Response:** Trump focused on expanding and fortifying the U.S.-Mexico border wall. However, the statement is hyperbolic as the concept of wall-building is not novel, and his administration's efforts were part of a continuation of previous border security measures.

Trumpism: "I know more about renewables than any human being on Earth."

- **Date:** April 2, 2019
- **Situation:** Remarks during a meeting on energy policy
- **Correct Response:** This is an exaggerated claim. Renewable energy is a complex field that requires expertise in technology, environmental science, and policy, typically studied and developed by experts and scientists over many years.

Trumpism: "We've done the best job of any country on the coronavirus."

- **Date:** August 4, 2020
- **Situation:** Remarks during a press briefing
- **Correct Response:** The U.S. faced significant challenges in

managing the COVID-19 pandemic, including high rates of infection and deaths compared to other developed countries. This statement does not align with the struggles faced by healthcare systems and the critical public health responses.

Trumpism: "We brought back manufacturing to the United States."

- **Date:** September 28, 2020
- **Situation:** Remarks at a campaign event
- **Correct Response:** While some manufacturing jobs returned due to policy changes and trade agreements, the broader trend of manufacturing in the U.S. shows a complex picture influenced by automation and global economic forces. The sector has not fully rebounded to historical highs.

Trumpism: "We have achieved energy independence."

- **Date:** November 9, 2019
- **Situation:** Remarks during a rally
- **Correct Response:** The U.S. has made significant strides towards reducing its dependence on foreign oil and has become a net exporter of energy. However, it still imports oil, and energy independence in the absolute sense remains complex and not fully realized.

Trumpism: "We built the greatest military in the world."

- **Date:** February 4, 2020
- **Situation:** Remarks during the State of the Union Address
- **Correct Response:** The U.S. military has long been considered the world's most powerful, with ongoing investment and technological advancements. The claim of "building" the greatest military overlooks the continuous efforts and resources allocated across many administrations.

Trumpism: "I've achieved peace in the Middle East."

- **Date:** September 15, 2020
- **Situation:** Remarks after the signing of the Abraham Accords
- **Correct Response:** While the Abraham Accords represented a significant diplomatic achievement, facilitating normalization of relations between Israel and several Arab nations, it is not accurate to claim that these agreements alone have achieved peace throughout the Middle East, a region with ongoing conflicts and complexities.

Trumpism: "We have the best economy ever because of my tax cuts."

- **Date:** February 5, 2020
- **Situation:** Remarks during the State of the Union Address
- **Correct Response:** The tax cuts implemented in 2017 helped stimulate economic growth and contributed to low unemployment rates prior to the COVID-19 pandemic. However, claiming the "best economy ever" overlooks historical periods of stronger proportional growth and the contributions of other economic factors.

Trumpism: "Nobody has done more for women than I have."

- **Date:** October 26, 2020
- **Situation:** Remarks at a campaign rally
- **Correct Response:** While Trump's administration supported various initiatives that impacted women, such as small business loans through the PPP and certain health care policies, the assertion of doing more for women than any other president overlooks significant historical achievements like the women's suffrage movement supported by other administrations.

Trumpism: "I know more about wind than you do."

- **Date:** September 26, 2019
- **Situation:** Remarks during a press briefing
- **Correct Response:** This claim was made in the context of criticizing wind energy, where Trump often repeated incorrect assertions about its reliability and environmental impact. Expertise in wind energy involves complex knowledge of engineering, environmental science, and energy policy.

Trumpism: "We're the greatest country in the history of countries."

- **Date:** July 3, 2020
- **Situation:** Remarks during an Independence Day celebration
- **Correct Response:** This is a patriotic expression common in political rhetoric. It is subjective and reflects national pride rather than an objective measurement against other nations' histories and achievements.

Trumpism: "The world respects us again. Believe me."

- **Date:** May 20, 2017
- **Situation:** Remarks during a state visit overseas
- **Correct Response:** International respect can be measured in various ways, including diplomatic relations, leadership in global crises, and adherence to international agreements. While some allies welcomed Trump's assertive leadership style, others expressed concern over his approach to international relations and treaties.

Trumpism: "I've signed more bills than any president ever."

- **Date:** July 17, 2017
- **Situation:** Remarks during a Cabinet meeting
- **Correct Response:** By the date of this statement, Trump had not signed more legislation than all other presidents at the same point in their presidencies. Historical records show that other presidents,

such as Franklin D. Roosevelt, signed a greater number of bills in their first six months in office.

Trumpism: "We have done an incredible job environmentally."

- **Date:** August 21, 2019
- **Situation:** Remarks during a speech
- **Correct Response:** Trump's administration rolled back numerous environmental protections, which critics argue harmed the U.S.'s environmental progress, particularly in terms of air and water quality and greenhouse gas emissions. The claim contrasts with the views of many environmental groups.

Trumpism: "We have the lowest Black unemployment in history."

- **Date:** February 4, 2019
- **Situation:** Remarks during the State of the Union Address
- **Correct Response:** Before the pandemic, Black unemployment in the U.S. did reach its lowest level since such records began in 1972. However, it's important to note that the decline began during the Obama administration, and disparities in employment rates between Black workers and other groups remained.

Trumpism: "We built the most powerful economy in the history of the world."

- **Date:** October 22, 2020
- **Situation:** Remarks during a presidential debate
- **Correct Response:** This statement about the U.S. economy prior to the pandemic is an example of hyperbole. While the economy was strong, whether it was the most powerful in the history of the world is subjective and dependent on specific economic metrics and comparisons.

Trumpism: "I made the U.S. the number one producer of oil and natural gas in the world."

- **Date:** October 9, 2020
- **Situation:** Remarks during a campaign rally
- **Correct Response:** The U.S. did become the leading producer of oil and natural gas, a milestone largely achieved due to technological advances like fracking. However, this status was reached during the Obama administration, and Trump's policies further supported the expansion of production.

Trumpism: "We have the best unemployment numbers in history."

- **Date:** January 14, 2020
- **Situation:** Remarks at a campaign event
- **Correct Response:** Before the pandemic, the U.S. did achieve historically low unemployment rates across various demographics, continuing a trend that began during the recovery from the 2008 financial crisis. However, "best" is subjective and must be viewed in context of the economic cycle.

Trumpism: "I protected pre-existing conditions."

- **Date:** February 4, 2020
- **Situation:** Remarks during the State of the Union address
- **Correct Response:** Trump repeatedly claimed to support protections for people with pre-existing conditions. However, his administration supported efforts to repeal the Affordable Care Act (ACA), which would have weakened those protections if no alternative plan was established.

Trumpism: "I am the most pro-Israel president ever."

- **Date:** August 17, 2020

- **Situation:** Remarks at a campaign rally
- **Correct Response:** Trump's administration took several actions that were strongly in favor of Israeli interests, including moving the U.S. Embassy to Jerusalem and recognizing Israeli sovereignty over the Golan Heights. These actions were significant but whether he is the "most" pro-Israel is subjective and depends on criteria for measurement.

Trumpism: "We killed ISIS."

- **Date:** January 28, 2020
- **Situation:** Remarks at a rally
- **Correct Response:** Trump's administration did oversee military operations that led to significant defeats for ISIS, including the death of its leader, Abu Bakr al-Baghdadi. However, declaring ISIS entirely defeated is misleading as the organization still has active cells and continues to pose a threat.

Trumpism: "We've got the cleanest air, the cleanest water we've ever had."

- **Date:** November 4, 2019
- **Situation:** Remarks at a campaign rally
- **Correct Response:** While U.S. air and water quality have improved over decades, Trump's administration rolled back several environmental regulations, which some experts argue could undermine long-term air and water quality. The claim does not reflect the ongoing environmental challenges and the nuanced state of natural resources.

Trumpism: "I built the strongest economy in the history of the world."

- **Date:** October 22, 2020
- **Situation:** Remarks during a presidential debate

- **Correct Response:** This statement reflects Trump's interpretation of economic indicators pre-pandemic, such as GDP growth and unemployment rates. While the economy was strong, the claim of it being the strongest in world history is an exaggeration and lacks historical and global context.

Trumpism: "We've rebuilt our military."

- **Date:** November 11, 2020
- **Situation:** Remarks on Veterans Day
- **Correct Response:** The U.S. military budget increased under Trump, funding new equipment and pay raises for troops. However, the U.S. military has consistently been well-funded and technologically advanced, making the term "rebuilt" more reflective of ongoing maintenance and enhancement rather than a complete overhaul.

Trumpism: "I've done more for veterans than any president in history."

- **Date:** May 25, 2019
- **Situation:** Remarks during a Memorial Day speech
- **Correct Response:** Trump signed significant legislation affecting veterans, including the VA MISSION Act. While these are notable achievements, whether they constitute "more than any president" is debatable, especially considering comprehensive reforms by other presidents.

Trumpism: "America is winning again like never before."

- **Date:** February 4, 2019
- **Situation:** Remarks during the State of the Union address
- **Correct Response:** This phrase is emblematic of Trump's optimistic portrayal of his administration's policies and achievements. However, "winning" is subjective and can vary

widely depending on the area of policy and the metrics used to measure success.

Trumpism: "I've created the best job numbers in history."

- **Date:** July 5, 2018
- **Situation:** Remarks during a press briefing
- **Correct Response:** While the U.S. experienced historically low unemployment rates prior to the COVID-19 pandemic, attributing these outcomes solely to Trump's policies overlooks broader economic trends and recovery efforts that began before his presidency. Moreover, "best" is subjective depending on metrics like job quality and inclusion of all demographics.

Trumpism: "We're respected all over the world again."

- **Date:** September 25, 2020
- **Situation:** Remarks at a campaign event
- **Correct Response:** International views on U.S. leadership varied significantly during Trump's presidency. Some global leaders praised his directness and policy shifts, while others expressed concerns about unpredictability and withdrawal from international agreements like the Paris Climate Accord and the Iran Nuclear Deal.

Trumpism: "I solved North Korea."

- **Date:** June 30, 2019
- **Situation:** Remarks after meeting Kim Jong-un
- **Correct Response:** Trump's engagement with North Korean leader Kim Jong-un marked a significant diplomatic effort. However, claiming to have "solved" North Korea is an overstatement, as the peninsula remains nuclear-armed, and significant diplomatic and security challenges persist.

Trumpism: "We have the biggest tax cuts in history."

- **Date:** January 30, 2019
- **Situation:** Remarks during an interview
- **Correct Response:** The Tax Cuts and Jobs Act of 2017 was significant, but not the largest in U.S. history by several measures, including as a percentage of GDP and in terms of overall impact on tax rates. Larger cuts have been enacted in the past, such as those under Presidents Ronald Reagan and John F. Kennedy.

Trumpism: "Nobody has done more for people with disabilities than me."

- **Date:** August 13, 2020
- **Situation:** Remarks during a White House event
- **Correct Response:** This claim is difficult to substantiate. While Trump's administration made some regulatory changes affecting people with disabilities, comprehensive policies and significant legislation like the Americans with Disabilities Act (ADA) have had broader and more profound impacts.

Trumpism: "We built the greatest border wall."

- **Date:** December 17, 2020
- **Situation:** Remarks during a visit to the border
- **Correct Response:** The Trump administration significantly increased the construction of barriers along the U.S.-Mexico border. However, much of this construction replaced existing barriers rather than expanding new areas of the wall. The effectiveness and impact of the wall continue to be debated.

Trumpism: "I've achieved more than any other President in the first three years."

- **Date:** February 4, 2020
- **Situation:** Remarks during the State of the Union address
- **Correct Response:** Trump's administration had several legislative and policy successes, but this claim is highly subjective and depends on the criteria used for measuring presidential achievements. Many presidents have had impactful first terms with substantial legislative and international accomplishments.

Trumpism: "Our military was depleted, but I have rebuilt it."

- **Date:** October 26, 2020
- **Situation:** Remarks during a campaign event
- **Correct Response:** The notion that the U.S. military was "depleted" is often used rhetorically. The U.S. has consistently had the world's most powerful military. Increases in spending under Trump continued a long tradition of robust military funding.

Trumpism: "I made America great again."

- **Date:** November 2, 2020
- **Situation:** Remarks during a campaign rally
- **Correct Response:** "Make America Great Again" was Trump's campaign slogan, reflecting his promise to improve various aspects of U.S. domestic and foreign policy. Whether America was made "great" again is highly subjective, varying widely based on political perspectives and specific policy outcomes.

Trumpism: "I have done more for Christianity than any president that's ever lived."

- **Date:** September 9, 2020
- **Situation:** Remarks during an interview
- **Correct Response:** While Trump implemented policies supported by many evangelical Christians, such as appointing conservative

judges and advocating for religious freedoms, this claim exaggerates his impact compared to presidents like Jimmy Carter, who was deeply involved in religious activities, or Ronald Reagan and George W. Bush, who both had significant relationships with the Christian community. The comparison lacks a clear metric for measurement.

Trumpism: "We've secured the borders like nobody's ever done before."

- **Date:** October 28, 2020
- **Situation:** Remarks during a campaign rally
- **Correct Response:** Trump's administration made significant efforts to strengthen border security, including expanding physical barriers. However, border security is a complex issue involving technology, personnel, and legal frameworks. The effectiveness and unprecedented nature of these efforts are debatable, with illegal crossings and asylum requests reflecting ongoing challenges.

Trumpism: "We have the cleanest air and cleanest water on the planet."

- **Date:** June 18, 2020
- **Situation:** Remarks during an environmental roundtable
- **Correct Response:** The U.S. ranks well in some environmental metrics but is not the absolute leader globally in either air or water quality. Countries like Finland, Iceland, and Sweden typically score higher in environmental performance indexes.

Trumpism: "I rebuilt the FBI."

- **Date:** May 17, 2019
- **Situation:** Remarks during a press conference
- **Correct Response:** Trump's claim to have "rebuilt" the FBI is not supported by clear evidence. While he appointed new leadership, such as Director Christopher Wray, the structure, function, and

integrity of the FBI have remained consistent with its long-standing role as a federal law enforcement agency.

Trumpism: "I'm the best thing that ever happened to Puerto Rico."

- **Date:** August 2, 2019
- **Situation:** Remarks during a White House briefing
- **Correct Response:** Trump's administration faced significant criticism for its handling of the aftermath of Hurricane Maria in Puerto Rico, particularly regarding the speed and adequacy of aid. This statement is seen as controversial and insensitive by critics, especially given the ongoing recovery challenges on the island.

Trumpism: "We've made America wealthy again."

- **Date:** October 13, 2020
- **Situation:** Remarks at a campaign event
- **Correct Response:** Economic growth occurred during Trump's presidency until the COVID-19 pandemic, benefiting certain sectors and income groups. However, wealth disparity remains a significant issue, and the assertion overlooks the uneven distribution of economic gains.

Trumpism: "I ended the war in Afghanistan."

- **Date:** November 26, 2020
- **Situation:** Remarks during a Thanksgiving message
- **Correct Response:** While Trump reduced U.S. troop levels in Afghanistan and negotiated with the Taliban, he did not end the conflict entirely. The situation remained complex with ongoing violence and peace talks still in progress.

Trumpism: "We have the greatest economy in the world."

- **Date:** September 3, 2020
- **Situation:** Remarks during a press briefing
- **Correct Response:** The U.S. economy is one of the largest and most dynamic, but using the term "greatest" is subjective and depends on various metrics including GDP, innovation, and standard of living. Additionally, the economic impact of the COVID-19 pandemic challenged this assertion.

Trumpism: "I've been the most transparent president in history."

- **Date:** May 31, 2019
- **Situation:** Remarks to the press
- **Correct Response:** Trump's refusal to release his tax returns and his administration's handling of certain information requests contradicted this claim. Previous presidents have engaged in more open practices, such as routinely releasing tax information and detailed health reports.

Trumpism: "America is respected again."

- **Date:** November 4, 2020
- **Situation:** Remarks during a campaign rally
- **Correct Response:** While some policies under Trump's administration were praised by certain allies for their assertiveness, surveys from global perspectives indicate a decline in views of the U.S. and its leadership during his term, challenging the notion of universal respect.

Trumpism: "I have the most loyal people."

- **Date:** February 23, 2016
- **Situation:** Remarks during a campaign rally
- **Correct Response:** While Trump's base has demonstrated strong loyalty, measuring the "most loyal" is inherently subjective. Loyalty

can vary significantly across different political figures and is influenced by numerous factors including political, social, and economic contexts.

Trumpism: "We brought back millions of jobs."

- **Date:** August 17, 2020
- **Situation:** Remarks at a campaign event
- **Correct Response:** Following initial job losses due to the COVID-19 pandemic, there was a significant rebound as businesses reopened. However, the overall U.S. employment numbers still reflected substantial net losses compared to pre-pandemic levels at this point.

Trumpism: "I am the chosen one."

- **Date:** August 21, 2019
- **Situation:** Remarks during a press briefing
- **Correct Response:** This statement was made while discussing trade with China and appeared to be partly in jest. However, it reflects Trump's often grandiose portrayal of his role in addressing international trade issues.

Trumpism: "We're the number one energy producer in the world."

- **Date:** September 10, 2020
- **Situation:** Remarks at a campaign rally
- **Correct Response:** The U.S. became the world's largest producer of oil and natural gas during the Trump administration, a status achieved towards the end of the Obama administration due to the shale revolution and innovations in drilling technology.

Trumpism: "Nobody has ever done what I've done for the military."

- **Date:** November 11, 2020
- **Situation:** Remarks on Veterans Day
- **Correct Response:** While Trump increased military spending and initiated some veteran policy reforms, many presidents have made significant contributions to the military and veterans, including large-scale military build-ups and comprehensive reforms in veteran care.

Trumpism: "I made the VA great again."

- **Date:** October 15, 2020
- **Situation:** Remarks during a town hall
- **Correct Response:** Trump signed the VA MISSION Act, improving some aspects of veteran healthcare and expanding options. However, challenges at the VA persisted, including issues with access to care and bureaucratic inefficiencies.

Trumpism: "We have the best technology in the world."

- **Date:** December 12, 2019
- **Situation:** Remarks at a technology conference
- **Correct Response:** The U.S. is a leader in many areas of technology, especially in software, internet services, and biotechnology. However, leadership in technology is dynamic, with other countries also excelling in various tech sectors.

Trumpism: "I stopped North Korea from starting a war."

- **Date:** June 30, 2019
- **Situation:** Remarks after a meeting with Kim Jong-un
- **Correct Response:** Trump's engagement with North Korea led to a reduction in immediate tensions, particularly regarding missile tests. However, the claim of preventing a war oversimplifies the complex geopolitical dynamics on the Korean Peninsula.

Trumpism: "We built the strongest border in our history."

- **Date:** October 26, 2020
- **Situation:** Remarks during a campaign event
- **Correct Response:** The Trump administration significantly increased security measures along the southern border, including constructing additional barriers. Whether this constitutes the "strongest border" in U.S. history is subjective and depends on the metrics used to evaluate border security effectiveness.

Trumpism: "America is the greatest country in the world."

- **Date:** July 4, 2020
- **Situation:** Remarks during Fourth of July celebrations
- **Correct Response:** This patriotic statement is common among U.S. politicians. While many Americans may agree with this sentiment, "greatest" is subjective and can be assessed differently based on various criteria such as freedom, economic strength, social justice, and quality of life.

Trumpism: "I fixed the economy."

- **Date:** November 3, 2020
- **Situation:** Remarks during a campaign rally
- **Correct Response:** The U.S. economy experienced growth during the early years of Trump's presidency, continuing an upward trend that began during the Obama administration. However, the COVID-19 pandemic caused a severe economic downturn, and while there was some recovery, the situation was complex and ongoing at the time of the statement.

Trumpism: "We have eliminated ISIS."

- **Date:** October 27, 2019

- **Situation:** Remarks after the death of ISIS leader Abu Bakr al-Baghdadi
- **Correct Response:** The Trump administration oversaw military operations that significantly weakened ISIS, including the operation that resulted in the death of its leader. However, experts caution that ISIS remains a threat with decentralized cells that can still carry out attacks globally.

Trumpism: "We've got the biggest navy in the world."

- **Date:** May 28, 2020
- **Situation:** Remarks during a shipyard visit
- **Correct Response:** The United States Navy is indeed one of the largest and most capable naval forces globally, a status it has maintained for decades due to sustained investment in shipbuilding and technological advancement.

Trumpism: "Nobody has ever built an economy like I've built."

- **Date:** July 2, 2020
- **Situation:** Remarks at a White House briefing
- **Correct Response:** The U.S. economy was robust prior to the pandemic, with significant job growth and stock market gains. However, claiming no one has ever built an economy like this overlooks historical economic booms under other administrations and the role of global economic factors.

Trumpism: "I am the most patriotic president."

- **Date:** July 4, 2021
- **Situation:** Remarks during Independence Day celebrations
- **Correct Response:** Patriotism is subjective, and while Trump often expressed strong nationalistic sentiments, measuring the patriotism of a president is inherently personal and not

quantifiable.

Trumpism: "We're leading in all the polls."

- **Date:** September 30, 2020
- **Situation:** Remarks during a presidential debate
- **Correct Response:** At the time of these remarks, polling data showed Trump trailing behind his opponent in many national polls and key battleground states. His statement did not reflect the broader trends indicated by most major polling organizations.

Trumpism: "I brought back NASA from being closed."

- **Date:** October 11, 2020
- **Situation:** Remarks during a campaign rally
- **Correct Response:** NASA was never closed, although it faced budget constraints and shifts in mission focus over the years. Trump's administration did prioritize space exploration, including funding for the Artemis program to return to the Moon.

Trumpism: "We're the envy of the world with our economy."

- **Date:** August 5, 2020
- **Situation:** Remarks during a press briefing
- **Correct Response:** While the U.S. economy has been a global leader in many respects, using the term "envy of the world" is hyperbolic and overlooks the economic challenges and inequalities present within the country.

Trumpism: "I've rebuilt our relationships with our allies."

- **Date:** June 10, 2019
- **Situation:** Remarks during a state visit
- **Correct Response:** Trump's approach to foreign policy was mixed,

with some allies expressing concerns over his unilateral actions and rhetoric. While he claimed to have strengthened alliances, some traditional alliances were strained during his tenure.

Trumpism: "I am the hardest working president in history."

- **Date:** May 3, 2020
- **Situation:** Tweet
- **Correct Response:** Work ethic and dedication are subjective qualities that are difficult to measure across presidencies. While Trump claimed to work tirelessly, his schedule often included significant "executive time" and frequent golf outings, which critics cited as evidence to the contrary.

Trumpism: "We've had the best stock market in history under my administration."

- **Date:** January 5, 2020
- **Situation:** Remarks during a campaign event
- **Correct Response:** The stock market did reach new highs during Trump's presidency, continuing an upward trend that began in March 2009. However, market performance alone is not a complete indicator of economic health, and attributing it solely to presidential influence overlooks broader economic forces.

Trumpism: "Under my leadership, America achieved energy independence."

- **Date:** September 29, 2020
- **Situation:** Remarks during a presidential debate
- **Correct Response:** The U.S. became a net exporter of oil and natural gas for the first time in decades during Trump's presidency. However, energy independence is complex, involving not just production but also geopolitical and market dynamics; the U.S.

still imports oil.

Trumpism: "I built the greatest economy in the history of the world."

- **Date:** October 22, 2020
- **Situation:** Remarks during a presidential debate
- **Correct Response:** While the U.S. economy was strong before the COVID-19 pandemic, the claim of building the greatest economy in world history is an exaggeration and overlooks other periods of strong economic performance both in the U.S. and in other countries.

Trumpism: "No president has ever cut taxes like I have."

- **Date:** April 15, 2019
- **Situation:** Remarks during a tax roundtable
- **Correct Response:** Trump's Tax Cuts and Jobs Act of 2017 significantly reduced corporate and individual tax rates. However, larger tax cuts have been implemented in the past, such as those during the Reagan administration.

Trumpism: "We've done more testing than any other country in the world."

- **Date:** July 21, 2020
- **Situation:** Remarks during a press briefing
- **Correct Response:** While the U.S. conducted a large number of COVID-19 tests, when adjusted for population, several countries had conducted more tests per capita. The effectiveness of testing also depends on the speed of processing and accessibility of testing.

Trumpism: "I've appointed more federal judges than any president in history."

- **Date:** November 4, 2020
- **Situation:** Remarks at a campaign rally
- **Correct Response:** Trump appointed a significant number of federal judges, including three Supreme Court Justices, but he did not appoint more judges than all other presidents. Several presidents, including George Washington and Franklin D. Roosevelt, appointed more due to new courts being established or existing ones expanded.

Trumpism: "We're the best at fighting the coronavirus."

- **Date:** May 5, 2020
- **Situation:** Remarks during a factory visit
- **Correct Response:** This claim conflicts with the U.S. having one of the highest rates of COVID-19 infections and deaths globally at the time. Effective pandemic management is complex and involves testing, contact tracing, medical infrastructure, and public compliance with health guidelines.

Trumpism: "We have the lowest Black unemployment in history because of my policies."

- **Date:** June 19, 2020
- **Situation:** Remarks during a Juneteenth event
- **Correct Response:** Black unemployment reached historic lows prior to the pandemic, continuing a downward trend that began during the Obama administration. While economic policies can influence employment rates, attributing these changes solely to one administration does not account for broader economic trends.

Trumpism: "I saved millions of lives with my COVID-19 response."

- **Date:** October 13, 2020
- **Situation:** Remarks during a campaign rally

- **Correct Response:** While measures like travel bans may have delayed the spread of the virus, the overall U.S. response to COVID-19 faced significant criticism regarding testing delays, mixed messaging on masks, and lack of a coordinated federal response.

Trumpism: "I passed the biggest tax cuts and reforms in American history."

- **Date:** January 30, 2018
- **Situation:** Remarks during the State of the Union address
- **Correct Response:** While the Tax Cuts and Jobs Act of 2017 was significant, it was not the largest tax cut in American history. Larger cuts have been enacted under Presidents Ronald Reagan and John F. Kennedy in terms of total dollars adjusted for inflation and as a percentage of the GDP.

Trumpism: "We built the strongest economy anyone has ever seen."

- **Date:** September 29, 2020
- **Situation:** Remarks during the first presidential debate
- **Correct Response:** The U.S. economy was experiencing strong growth and low unemployment rates before the COVID-19 pandemic. However, the assertion that it was the strongest economy "anyone has ever seen" is subjective and overlooks other historical periods of economic strength both in the U.S. and globally.

Trumpism: "I've done more for healthcare than any other president."

- **Date:** October 22, 2020
- **Situation:** Remarks during the second presidential debate
- **Correct Response:** Trump's administration made efforts to dismantle the Affordable Care Act and took steps to reduce drug

prices, among other initiatives. However, the claim of doing more for healthcare than any other president does not account for comprehensive healthcare reforms like those introduced by Presidents Lyndon B. Johnson (Medicare and Medicaid) and Barack Obama (Affordable Care Act).

Trumpism: "We have the best military in the world, and we've rebuilt it."

- **Date:** November 11, 2020
- **Situation:** Remarks on Veterans Day
- **Correct Response:** The U.S. military is indeed among the most capable and well-funded in the world. While Trump increased defense spending, the military has been continually modernized and maintained by successive administrations, so the notion of it being entirely "rebuilt" is an exaggeration.

Trumpism: "I've accomplished more than any other president in the first three years."

- **Date:** February 4, 2020
- **Situation:** Remarks during the State of the Union address
- **Correct Response:** Trump's administration saw significant legislative achievements and judicial appointments. However, quantifying accomplishments is subjective, and various presidents have had impactful first terms with substantial legislative, economic, and foreign policy achievements.

Trumpism: "We ended the war on American energy."

- **Date:** October 13, 2020
- **Situation:** Remarks during a campaign rally
- **Correct Response:** Trump's policies focused on deregulating the energy sector and promoting fossil fuels. However, describing previous regulatory efforts as a "war" on American energy is a

rhetorical device that frames environmental regulations as overly restrictive.

Trumpism: "I've been the best president for women."

- **Date:** October 27, 2020
- **Situation:** Remarks at a campaign event
- **Correct Response:** Trump's administration implemented policies impacting women, including appointing women to key positions. However, his claim of being the best president for women is contested, particularly given his administration's policies on reproductive rights and healthcare.

Trumpism: "We turned around the U.S. auto industry."

- **Date:** September 10, 2020
- **Situation:** Remarks during a campaign rally in Michigan
- **Correct Response:** The U.S. auto industry recovered significantly after the 2008 financial crisis, largely due to the auto bailout initiated during the Obama administration. Trump's policies, such as renegotiating trade agreements, impacted the industry, but the turnaround began well before his presidency.

Trumpism: "We've got the best employment numbers in history."

- **Date:** February 6, 2019
- **Situation:** Remarks at a White House event
- **Correct Response:** Prior to the pandemic, the U.S. did achieve historically low unemployment rates. However, this trend began during the recovery from the 2008 financial crisis, and attributing these figures solely to Trump's policies overlooks the cyclical nature of economic recoveries.

Trumpism: "No one has done more for the middle class than me."

- **Date:** July 17, 2020
- **Situation:** Remarks during a campaign event
- **Correct Response:** Trump's tax reforms and economic policies benefited certain segments of the middle class, but the overall impact on the middle class is mixed, with debates about the benefits of his tax policies skewing toward wealthier individuals and corporations.

Trumpism: "I am the greatest jobs president that God ever created."

- **Date:** June 16, 2015
- **Situation:** Remarks during his presidential campaign announcement
- **Correct Response:** While job growth continued during Trump's presidency, peaking before the COVID-19 pandemic, the claim of being the greatest jobs president is subjective. The U.S. economy was already in a phase of recovery and job creation that began under the Obama administration.

Trumpism: "I've signed the biggest Veterans Affairs reform in history."

- **Date:** June 23, 2017
- **Situation:** Remarks during the signing of the VA Accountability Act
- **Correct Response:** The VA Accountability and Whistleblower Protection Act was an important piece of legislation aimed at increasing accountability within the Veterans Affairs offices. While significant, whether it is the "biggest" reform could be debated, as the Veterans Health Administration underwent substantial reforms and expansions under previous administrations.

Trumpism: "We've achieved the most secure border in U.S. history."

- **Date:** October 28, 2020

- **Situation:** Remarks during a campaign rally
- **Correct Response:** Trump's administration took several measures to enhance border security, including constructing additional barriers. However, the effectiveness and implications of these measures continue to be debated, and the claim of achieving the most secure border in history is difficult to measure objectively.

Trumpism: "We're the economic envy of the entire world."

- **Date:** July 27, 2018
- **Situation:** Remarks during a press conference
- **Correct Response:** At various times during Trump's presidency, the U.S. economy showed strong performance indicators. However, being the "economic envy" is a subjective assessment, and other nations also exhibit strong economic metrics that could be envied.

Trumpism: "Our military is the strongest it's ever been."

- **Date:** August 9, 2019
- **Situation:** Remarks at a fundraising event
- **Correct Response:** The U.S. military is continually updated with advanced technology and strong personnel training. While the military has seen budget increases under Trump, it has been among the world's strongest for decades due to ongoing investment and innovation.

Trumpism: "We have the best testing in the world for COVID-19."

- **Date:** May 11, 2020
- **Situation:** Remarks during a press briefing
- **Correct Response:** The U.S. conducted a high volume of COVID-19 tests, but faced issues with test availability, delays in results, and testing coverage compared to other countries that

implemented more comprehensive and efficient testing protocols early in the pandemic.

Trumpism: "I've built the greatest economy in the world."

- **Date:** October 16, 2019
- **Situation:** Remarks during a campaign rally
- **Correct Response:** While the U.S. economy was performing strongly in terms of GDP growth and unemployment rates before the pandemic, the global ranking can vary based on different economic indicators. Such a claim oversimplifies the complex factors that contribute to a national economy's strength.

Trumpism: "We did a phenomenal job on the pandemic."

- **Date:** September 10, 2020
- **Situation:** Remarks during a campaign event
- **Correct Response:** The U.S. government's response to the COVID-19 pandemic has been widely criticized for various aspects, including inconsistent messaging on mask-wearing and a lack of a coordinated national testing strategy. This claim contrasts with the assessments of many public health experts.

Trumpism: "I brought back the auto industry."

- **Date:** June 18, 2020
- **Situation:** Remarks during a campaign event in Michigan
- **Correct Response:** While Trump's policies aimed at revitalizing manufacturing, including the auto industry, by renegotiating trade agreements and imposing tariffs on foreign goods, the U.S. auto industry's recovery began well before his presidency, following the post-2008 financial crisis bailouts. His influence was more about continuation and policy adjustments rather than a full-scale revival from decline.

Trumpism: "We built the strongest economy ever."

- **Date:** August 17, 2020
- **Situation:** Remarks at a campaign rally
- **Correct Response:** Prior to the COVID-19 pandemic, the U.S. economy did exhibit strong growth, continuing a trend that began during the recovery from the Great Recession. However, stating it as the "strongest economy ever" overlooks historical economic booms under other presidents and doesn't account for all economic indicators, such as income inequality and overall wealth distribution.

Trumpism: "I achieved the most secure border in our history."

- **Date:** September 10, 2020
- **Situation:** Remarks during a campaign rally in Arizona
- **Correct Response:** Trump's administration implemented strict immigration policies and expanded physical barriers at the southern border. While these measures may have reduced illegal crossings, the claim of achieving the "most secure border in our history" is subjective and depends on the metrics used for measurement.

Trumpism: "I saved millions of lives during the pandemic."

- **Date:** October 22, 2020
- **Situation:** Remarks during the second presidential debate
- **Correct Response:** Trump often credited his decision to restrict travel from China and Europe as saving lives during the COVID-19 pandemic. While these actions may have helped delay the spread, the overall U.S. response faced significant criticism for a lack of a cohesive national strategy, testing issues, and mixed messaging on public health guidelines.

Trumpism: "I made America respected again."

- **Date:** November 3, 2020
- **Situation:** Remarks on election night
- **Correct Response:** Trump's foreign policy was characterized by a "America First" approach, which included withdrawing from several international agreements and organizations. While this approach was praised by some for prioritizing American interests, it was criticized by others who felt it damaged traditional alliances and reduced U.S. standing on global issues.

Trumpism: "Nobody has reduced taxes like I have."

- **Date:** October 15, 2020
- **Situation:** Remarks at a town hall meeting
- **Correct Response:** Trump's administration implemented significant tax cuts, particularly for corporations and high-income individuals. However, historically, larger proportional tax reductions have been enacted, such as those under Presidents Ronald Reagan and John F. Kennedy.

Trumpism: "We created the greatest immigration system in the world."

- **Date:** June 22, 2020
- **Situation:** Remarks during a policy announcement
- **Correct Response:** Trump's administration made substantial changes to U.S. immigration policy, emphasizing border security and reducing legal immigration. While supporters praised these changes for enforcing laws and protecting American jobs, critics argued that the policies were overly restrictive and harmed the nation's image as a welcoming destination for immigrants.

Trumpism: "I built the best economy in history before the pandemic."

- **Date:** October 22, 2020
- **Situation:** Remarks during the final presidential debate
- **Correct Response:** The U.S. economy was performing well with low unemployment and steady GDP growth before the COVID-19 pandemic, continuing a trend that began during the recovery from the 2008 financial crisis. However, claims of building the "best economy in history" are subjective and overlook periods of equally robust or superior economic performance in the past.

Trumpism: "I have been the best president for African Americans, with the possible exception of Abraham Lincoln."

- **Date:** June 16, 2020
- **Situation:** Remarks at a roundtable discussion
- **Correct Response:** While Trump did implement some policies that benefited the African American community, such as criminal justice reform and funding for historically black colleges and universities, this claim overlooks significant advancements made by other presidents, notably Lyndon B. Johnson, who signed the Civil Rights Act and Voting Rights Act, which were transformative for civil rights in America.

Trumpism: "We have done a phenomenal job on the coronavirus."

- **Date:** September 10, 2020
- **Situation:** Remarks during a press briefing
- **Correct Response:** The response to the COVID-19 pandemic in the U.S. received mixed reviews. While the administration expedited vaccine development through Operation Warp Speed, it was criticized for its handling of testing, contact tracing, and consistent public health messaging. The U.S. experienced one of the highest infection and death rates globally.

Trumpism: "I passed the most comprehensive tax reform in history."

- **Date:** December 22, 2017
- **Situation:** Remarks after signing the Tax Cuts and Jobs Act
- **Correct Response:** The Tax Cuts and Jobs Act of 2017 did make significant changes to the tax code, including reducing the corporate tax rate and altering individual tax brackets. However, whether it was the most comprehensive reform is debatable, with major overhauls also enacted under Ronald Reagan and other presidents.

Trumpism: "We rebuilt the military from nothing."

- **Date:** October 19, 2020
- **Situation:** Remarks during a campaign rally
- **Correct Response:** The U.S. military is consistently one of the best-funded and technologically advanced in the world. Claims of rebuilding "from nothing" are exaggerated, as the military maintained high levels of readiness and capability before and during Trump's presidency, though his administration did increase defense spending.

Trumpism: "We have the lowest carbon emissions in years."

- **Date:** July 8, 2020
- **Situation:** Remarks during an energy policy discussion
- **Correct Response:** U.S. carbon emissions have declined over several years due to a variety of factors, including shifts from coal to natural gas and renewable energy sources. However, the U.S. remains one of the largest per capita emitters of carbon, and environmental policy changes under Trump's administration were often aimed at reducing regulations on fossil fuels.

Trumpism: "We created the best immigration system."

- **Date:** August 5, 2020
- **Situation:** Remarks during a press briefing
- **Correct Response:** The Trump administration implemented strict immigration policies, which included reducing the number of legal immigrants, increasing border security, and imposing travel bans from certain countries. While supporters argued these measures improved national security, critics claimed they were overly harsh and disrupted the lives of immigrants and their families.

Trumpism: "I have the highest approval ratings ever recorded."

- **Date:** August 24, 2020
- **Situation:** Tweet
- **Correct Response:** This statement is inaccurate. While Trump had solid approval ratings among Republicans, his overall approval ratings during his presidency were generally lower compared to past presidents, according to various polling data.

Trumpism: "Nobody has ever done a better job than I have on the economy."

- **Date:** May 13, 2020
- **Situation:** Remarks at a White House event
- **Correct Response:** This claim is highly subjective. While economic indicators like stock markets and unemployment were strong before the pandemic, attributing this solely to Trump's actions overlooks broader economic trends and the role of global economic conditions.

Trumpism: "I cut more regulations than any president in history."

- **Date:** November 24, 2020
- **Situation:** Remarks during a Cabinet meeting
- **Correct Response:** Trump's administration did prioritize

deregulation, particularly in the environmental and financial sectors. While he significantly reduced federal regulations, measuring these cuts against all historical presidencies is complex, as systematic tracking of regulatory actions across all administrations isn't uniformly detailed.

Trumpism: "I fixed our broken trade deals."

- **Date:** October 22, 2020
- **Situation:** Remarks during the final presidential debate
- **Correct Response:** Trump renegotiated several key trade agreements, including NAFTA, replacing it with the United States-Mexico-Canada Agreement (USMCA). His administration also engaged in significant trade disputes with China. While these new agreements brought changes, whether they "fixed" trade depends on perspective and economic outcomes, which are mixed.

Trumpism: "Under my administration, we achieved energy dominance."

- **Date:** September 8, 2020
- **Situation:** Remarks at a campaign event
- **Correct Response:** The U.S. became a net exporter of oil and natural gas during Trump's tenure, largely due to advancements in fracking and other extraction technologies. The term "energy dominance" can be interpreted in various ways, but it generally reflects increased U.S. influence in global energy markets.

Trumpism: "I built the greatest border wall ever seen."

- **Date:** August 18, 2020
- **Situation:** Remarks during a visit to the border wall
- **Correct Response:** Trump significantly expanded barriers along the U.S.-Mexico border. However, much of this construction replaced existing structures rather than being completely new. The

effectiveness and impact of the wall are subjects of ongoing debate.

Trumpism: "We ended the AIDS epidemic."

- **Date:** August 27, 2020
- **Situation:** Remarks during the Republican National Convention
- **Correct Response:** The Trump administration launched an initiative to significantly reduce new HIV infections in the United States by 2030. However, claiming to have ended the AIDS epidemic is premature and inaccurate, as the disease remains a significant public health issue both domestically and globally.

Trumpism: "I've done more for women than just about any president."

- **Date:** October 1, 2020
- **Situation:** Remarks during a campaign rally
- **Correct Response:** Trump's administration supported several initiatives impacting women, such as promoting women in STEM fields and supporting women entrepreneurs. However, his claim is contested by critics who point to actions and policies considered detrimental to women's rights and interests, particularly in healthcare and reproductive rights.

Trumpism: "We have rebuilt the U.S. military."

- **Date:** January 14, 2020
- **Situation:** Remarks at a rally
- **Correct Response:** Trump's administration increased military spending, focusing on modernization and readiness. However, the U.S. military has been continually maintained and modernized by successive administrations, and characterizing it as "rebuilt" suggests a recovery from a state of disrepair, which is not accurate.

Trumpism: "America is the most respected country again."

- **Date:** July 4, 2020
- **Situation:** Remarks during Fourth of July celebrations
- **Correct Response:** This claim is subjective. While some policies under Trump were applauded by certain international actors, others, particularly in Europe and among traditional allies, expressed concerns about his unilateral approach to global affairs and withdrawal from international agreements.

Conclusion

Donald Trump's use of definitive and superlative statements—often termed "Trumpisms"—reflects a communication style that is both assertive and unequivocal. These statements are not just remarks but are strategic tools used to frame his presidency in terms of unequivocal success and decisive action. This method of communication can have a profound impact on public discourse, shaping how policies are perceived by the public, influencing political allies and adversaries, and directing media narratives.

Impact on Public Discourse

Trump's definitive statements often present complex issues in black-and-white terms, simplifying nuanced policies into easily digestible sound bites. This approach can appeal to wide audiences by reducing the cognitive load required to understand intricate policy discussions. However, it also risks oversimplifying the challenges and underrepresenting the complexity of governmental operations and international relations. Such simplifications can polarize public opinion, entrenching divisions among those who either accept or reject these simplifications outright.

Influence on Political and Media Landscape

In the political arena, Trump's superlative use of language serves to assert dominance and project confidence. It positions him as a decisive leader unafraid to take bold actions. For allies, it can rally support and unify factions under broad, assertive goals. For adversaries, it challenges them to dispute these claims in a media environment that often prioritizes catchy, definitive statements over detailed policy analysis.

In the media landscape, these statements generate a significant amount of coverage, partly due to their bold nature and the ease with which they can be broadcast and discussed. Media outlets, whether supportive or critical, find such statements newsworthy, leading to extensive analysis, debate, and commentary. This continuous cycle amplifies Trump's presence in public discourse, keeping his policies and presidency in the constant view of the public eye.

Necessity for Contextualization

The need for contextualizing Trump's "Trumpisms" arises from the gap that often exists between the rhetorical simplicity of his statements and the layered realities of governance. Each claim—whether it regards economic achievements, military strength, or international standing—carries implications that extend beyond the immediate reaction they provoke. Historians, economists, policy analysts, and media must thus evaluate these claims against a backdrop of empirical data and historical context to provide a balanced understanding.

For instance, when Trump claims to have built the "greatest economy in history," this prompts economists to examine indicators such as GDP growth, employment rates, wage growth, and international trade balances. They must consider the economic trajectory inherited by his administration, the global economic climate, and the long-term sustainability of his policies.

Conclusion

In summary, Trump's frequent use of definitive and superlative statements is a deliberate rhetorical strategy that impacts the political and media landscape by simplifying complex issues and asserting unwavering confidence. While effective for rallying support and dominating media cycles, these statements require careful contextualization to ensure that public discourse and policy understanding are grounded in reality, not just rhetoric. This necessitates a vigilant and informed approach from those engaged in analyzing and communicating political information.

Don't miss out!

Visit the website below and you can sign up to receive emails whenever Adrian Rocquecliffe publishes a new book. There's no charge and no obligation.

https://books2read.com/r/B-A-LUNRB-KHMXE

Did you love *Trumpisms: Decoding the Rhetoric of Disruption*? Then you should read *How Well do you Know Your Candidate?*[1] by Adrian Rocquecliffe!

[2]

Making informed voting decisions is more important than ever. In "How Well Do You Know Your Candidates? " readers are guided step by step through the process of evaluating political candidates. This book helps voters understand the qualities that make a strong leader, recognize the impact of a candidate's past and present actions, and consider the importance of their future plans. It also dives into the dangers of extremism, the role of misinformation, and the influence of political parties on our choices. With practical tools for critical thinking and strategies to overcome biases, this book empowers readers to make thoughtful, well-informed decisions that truly reflect their values and contribute to a healthier democracy. Whether you're a seasoned voter or casting your ballot for the first time, this book is your essential guide to making every vote count.

---

1. https://books2read.com/u/38GXnr

2. https://books2read.com/u/38GXnr

Read more at https://www.makingamericagreataltogether.us/adrian_rocquecliffe.

Also by Adrian Rocquecliffe

Making America Great Altogether - Call to Action

Trump's Vision of MAGA- The Fallacy

Extra! Extra! Read All About It

Trump's Insurrection of the US Capitol

How Well do you Know Your Candidate?

Trumpisms: Decoding the Rhetoric of Disruption

The Republican Agenda: Undoing 200 Years of Democracy for a Dictatorship

Under the Iron Flag: A Family's Battle for Survival and Justice in Trump's America

Complimentary Orchiectomy with First Sexual Offense: Starting at the Top

The Gulf of America: Trump's Vision for a United Continent

Project 2026 USA: We the People, For the People, By the People

Watch for more at https://www.makingamericagreataltogether.us/adrian_rocquecliffe.

About the Author

Adrian Rocquecliffe's journey from a young boy navigating cultural divides to a successful entrepreneur and visionary leader exemplifies the American dream. His dedication to improving the country for future generations is a testament to his belief in the power of unity and collaboration. As he continues his work with "Making America Great Altogether," Adrian remains hopeful that his efforts will contribute to a better, more inclusive America when he retires.

Read more at https://www.makingamericagreataltogether.us/ adrian_rocquecliffe.

About the Publisher

Writers Sidekick Publishing is a key part of the Writers Sidekick Resource Hub. Writers Sidekick Publishing specializes in publishing anthologies that welcome submissions from both new and established authors, providing a platform to showcase their work and contribute to the literary world. Additionally, it produces exclusive books tailored to the needs of the Writers Sidekick Resource Hub community.